T0275045

LET MY PEOPLE LAUGH

GREATEST JEWISH JOKES OF ALL TIME!

BY SALVADOR LITVAK

Skyhorse Publishing

To my wife, Nina, who made me rehearse
every joke until I got it right.

I wasn't born funny, I married into it.

All Rights Reserved. No part of this book may be reproduced in any manner without the express written consent of the publisher, except in the case of brief excerpts in critical reviews or articles. All inquiries should be addressed to Skyhorse Publishing, 307 West 36th Street, 11th Floor, New York, NY 10018.

Skyhorse Publishing books may be purchased in bulk at special discounts for sales promotion, corporate gifts, fund-raising, or educational purposes. Special editions can also be created to specifications. For details, contact the Special Sales Department, Skyhorse Publishing, 307 West 36th Street, 11th Floor, New York, NY 10018 or info@skyhorsepublishing.com.

Skyhorse® and Skyhorse Publishing® are registered trademarks of Skyhorse Publishing, Inc.®, a Delaware corporation.

Visit our website at www.skyhorsepublishing.com.

10 9 8 7 6 5 4 3 2 1

Library of Congress Cataloging-in-Publication Data is available on file.

Print ISBN: 978-1-5107-8216-7
eBook ISBN: 978-1-5107-8220-4

Cover design by David Ter-Avanesyan

Printed in the United States of America

INTRODUCTION

Morry gets invited to the Friars Club for the first time. He's excited to join a table of old, famous comedians.

One of them says, "Fifteen," and everyone cracks up. Another says, "Forty-two," and again they all laugh.

Morry asks a member, "What's going on?"

"They've been doing this so long, they all know the same jokes. To save time, they numbered 'em."

"Oh, cool," says Morry, "I'll give that a try."

He stands up and says, "Nineteen!" The old comics stare at Morry. No one laughs. Embarrassed, he sits down and turns to the member.

"What happened?"

"You told it wrong."[1]

My pal, you are holding an historic joke book. Only one of the jokes contained herein is new.[2] Most have been around for decades, some for centuries. They've been told by our parents, collected by rabbis, adapted by comedians, and many have even been published, but until now they were never *numbered*.

---

1 Alternative punchline, "Some people can tell a joke, some can't."
2 Guess which and you can win a t-shirt at accidentaltalmudist.org/contact.

The numbers are not rankings. Who can say whether "The Big Wave" outranks "The Interfaith Conference?" And who cares? What matters isn't whether one joke is objectively funnier than another, but rather how you tell it and *when*.

This book isn't organized like other Jewish jokebooks: marriage, rabbis, chutzpah, etc. Rather, it's all about arming you with the right joke when you need it. I numbered them like the Friars' jokes so you can glance at the list on the next page and grab the greatest joke *for your situation*, whether it's a wedding toast, Shabbat dinner, golf outing or business meeting, and especially if someone volunteers you to give the dreaded fundraising speech. Many jokes work in multiple situations, and that's why they had to be numbered.

I love these jokes, and I've told them in every possible situation. I've screwed up the punchlines, told them to the wrong crowd, and brought them out at the wrong time. I've bombed, so you don't have to.

I've also adapted every joke for the modern ear, based on decades of experience as a public speaker, influencer, toast-maker, and golf buddy. So be confident, practice a few times before you deliver, and wow your friends with your poise and wit!

Ladies and gentlemen, let my people laugh!

GREATEST JEWISH JOKES FOR A . . .

WEDDING TOAST
12, 21, 24, 27, 39, 55, 73, 90, 145, 157

FUNDRAISING SPEECH
1, 15, 19, 23, 32, 45, 54, 63, 91, 95, 104, 112, 116, 119, 152, 156, 161

SERMON/TEACHING
1, 15, 19, 21, 23, 29, 34, 36, 39, 44, 59, 67, 81, 101, 108, 110, 116, 118, 124, 134, 159

GOLF COURSE
2, 3, 6, 16, 26, 28, 30, 33, 40, 42, 47, 49, 61, 64, 69, 82, 99, 139, 143, 154

KEYNOTE ADDRESS
15, 17, 19, 21, 26, 29, 48, 63, 65, 95, 99, 105, 112, 115, 120, 142, 149

FIRST DATE
19, 25, 29, 54, 129, 135

SHABBOS TABLE/HOLIDAY GATHERING
7, 8, 11, 12, 13, 18, 19, 21, 24, 31, 33, 37, 44, 45, 47, 48, 49, 51, 54, 56, 62, 67, 73, 83, 86, 98, 103, 119, 120, 123, 128, 130, 133, 135, 136, 149, 153

BAR/BAT MITZVAH
15, 19, 23, 29, 36, 39, 50, 59, 81, 89, 108, 112, 116, 124, 134, 159

ROAD TRIP
3, 5, 20, 29, 38, 47, 78, 85, 89, 110, 140, 151, 155, 160

BUSINESS MEETING
2, 9, 20, 26, 32, 49, 53, 61, 69, 74, 78, 104, 107, 143, 152

#1

CAPTURED BY CANNIBALS

A rabbi, a cantor, and a synagogue[3] president are flying to a conference when their plane crashes and they're captured by cannibals.

The chief cannibal says, "We're going to kill you and eat you, but we will give you one final wish."

The president says, "I've been working on my speech for the building fund for months. It's an hour long. I'd like to deliver that before I die."

The rabbi says, "I've been working on my sermon for Rosh Hashanah for months. It's two hours long. I'd like to deliver that before I die."

The cantor says, "Kill me first."

---

3   "Shul" is funnier than synagogue if your audience is Jewish enough.

#2

BEGGARS AT THE VATICAN

Two beggars ply their trade outside the Vatican.

One wears a large Star of David on a string around his neck. His basket contains a few pennies.

The other wears a large crucifix, and his basket overflows with cash.

A priest walks out of the Vatican and notices the two beggars. He takes pity on the one with meager earnings.

"Forgive me for intruding, but given where you are, maybe that Jewish star isn't the best choice . . . ?"

The beggar with the Jewish star turns to the beggar with the cross and says, "Moishy, look who's trying to teach us about marketing!"

#3

THE JEWISH SAMURAI

The Emperor needs a new Chief Samurai. After a proclamation is made far and wide, three finalists emerge for the prestigious position.

The first is a samurai from the south. He steps forward and opens a small box. A fly soars out—*zzzzzzzzzzz*. The samurai draws his sword, slices the air, and the fly falls dead, split in two.

The Emperor is impressed.

The second finalist is a ninja from the north. He steps forward and opens a tiny box. A gnat flies out—*neeeeeeeee*. The ninja draws his sword, *whoosh*, and the gnat falls dead, split in two.

The Emperor nods with satisfaction.

The third finalist is Shimmy Yankowitz from Crown Heights, Brooklyn. He steps forward and opens a cigar box. A bumblebee rises slowly—*jjjjjjjjjjjjjj*. Shimmy slices the air three times . . . and the bumble bee flies away.

The Emperor snorts, "Some samurai. The bee did not die."

"No, your majesty. The circumcision is not intended to kill."

#4

THE TOP HAT

Leibowitz is sitting at his dining room table, wearing only a top hat, when Greenbaum walks in.

"Why are you sitting here naked?"

"It's OK, nobody ever comes to visit."

"But why the hat?"

"Maybe somebody will come."

#5

WHO'S THE MOST FAMOUS PERSON?

In a kindergarten class, the teacher offers the kids $5 if they can name the most famous person who ever lived.

Little Sean O'Sullivan says, "Saint Patrick!"

The teacher says, "No, I'm sorry, Sean, that's not correct."

Little Jimmy Williams says, "Abraham Lincoln!"

"No, Jimmy, I'm afraid that's not the answer."

Little David Goldberg says, "It's Jesus!"

"That's right, David, you get the $5 prize!"

When he comes up to collect, the teacher says, "You know David, with you being Jewish and all, I was surprised you said Jesus."

"Yes, ma'am. In my heart I knew it was Moses, but business is business."

#6

RABBI'S SECRET

It's Yom Kippur.[4] The rabbi, who's addicted to golf, can't help himself. So, he goes out and plays a few holes before the service.

First hole, he makes a birdie.[5] Up in heaven, Moses turns to God and says, "You let him make a birdie on Yom Kippur?!"

God says, "Just watch."

On the second hole, the rabbi makes an eagle.[6] Moses frowns. He can't believe what he's seeing.

Then, on the third hole, the rabbi misses the green, hits a tree, gets a ridiculous bounce, and makes a hole-in-one.[7]

Moses turns to God with outrage. "Lord, what are You doing? He plays golf on Yim Kippur and you give him a birdie, an eagle, and a hole-in-one?!"

"Yes, but who's he going to tell?"

---

4   The Day of Atonement. No eating, bathing, lovemaking, or golf allowed.
5   A great score for an amateur golfer.
6   A rare and wonderful score for an amateur.
7   For most golfers, once in a lifetime. Add in the crazy bounce, and this is a story a golfer would recount for the rest of his life.

#7

THE FORTUNE TELLER

Feeling his days are numbered, the head of Hamas visits a psychic.

"Fortune teller, when will I die?"

"You will die on a Jewish holiday."

"Which? Hanukkah? Passover? Tell me, I need to know!"

"Don't worry. Any day you die will be a Jewish holiday."

#8

THE TELEVISION SET

A Hasidic Jew comes into an electronics store in Brooklyn and says, "I'd like to buy this TV."

"We don't sell TVs to Hasids."[8]

The Hasidic guy gets mad. He leaves the store, tucks his peyos[9] inside a baseball cap, changes his clothes and walks back in.

"I'd like to buy this TV."

"We don't sell TVs to Hasids."

Now he's furious. He storms out of the store and returns two weeks later: no beard, no peyos, and wearing hipster clothes.

"I'd like to buy this TV."

"How many times do I gotta tell you? We don't sell TVs to Hasids."

"How do you know I'm a Hasid?!"

"Because this is a microwave oven."

---

8   Many Hasidic Jews don't have TVs or smart phones in order to guard their eyes from inappropriate images.

9   Forelocks of hair, hanging down from his temples.

#9

THE NEWSPAPER

In Berlin in the 1930s, two old Jews are sitting on a park bench reading the newspaper. One reads a Yiddish paper, the other reads a German paper.

"How can you read that Nazi rag?"

"What do you mean? When I read the Yiddish papers, it's all about Jews deported, Jews insulted, Jews assaulted. When I read the Nazi paper, it says we own the banks, we own the media, we control everything . . . The news is much better!"

#10
CAR ACCIDENT

An old man is hit by a car.

An EMT dresses his wounds and places a neck brace on him.

"Sir, are you comfortable?"

"Meh, I make a living."

#11

MAX'S FINAL WORDS

Old Max Greenberg lies on his deathbed.

He croaks, "Is my wife Sara here?"

"Yes," she cries, "I'm here with you."

"Are my children here?"

"Yes, Max, your sons and your daughters are all here!"

"Are my grandchildren here?"

"Yes, Max, we're all here with you!"

And then Max Greenberg lifts his head one last time and says, "So why is the light on in the kitchen?"[10]

---

10 Alt: "So who's minding the store?"

#12

GENIE IN A BOTTLE

David and Karen have been married for seven years. They've been fighting and they know they need to work on their marriage, so they book a big vacation to Tahiti.

They arrive at the resort and it's beautiful, but on the first day they have a fight. David storms off and walks up the beach. He sees something buried in the sand and finds an old oil lamp. He wipes off the dirt and a genie appears.

"Thank you, master, for freeing me! I grant you one wish."

David realizes this is the opportunity of a lifetime. He pulls out his phone and opens Google Maps.

"This is the Middle East. Please make peace between Israel and all her neighbors."

"You think I haven't heard of the conflict? That is way too complicated for a wish. You need to wish for something reasonable."

David thinks about his fights with Karen and says, "OK. I wish to understand how women think."

The genie leans in close to David and says, "Show me that map again."

#13

THE RABBI IN HAWAII

Rabbi Goldfarb always had an urge to try pork, but he's never given in to it.

On vacation in Hawaii, he's incredibly tempted by the delicious-smelling suckling pig they bring out nightly during the luau at his resort.

I'm so far away from home. Who's gonna know? And he finally says yes to the waiter.

While he's waiting for it to arrive, he's shocked to see Mr. and Mrs. Rosenberg from his synagogue walking over.

"Rabbi Goldfarb, so good to see you! Imagine running into you here!"

Dreading the arrival of his entree, he tries to keep the conversation short, but it's no use. The waiter brings a steaming roast pig with an apple in its mouth, and places it in front of the rabbi.

The Rosenbergs look down at the pig and up at the rabbi. Rabbi Goldfarb stares back at them, then down at the pig.

"This resort is so over the top. Imagine, I ordered an apple and this is how it comes!"

#14

MAX'S CARDIOLOGIST

Max Goldberg goes to see his cardiologist. The doctor performs a long examination, and then says he'd like to speak to Mrs. Goldberg privately.

Max leaves the room, and his wife comes in.

"Mrs. Goldberg, your husband's coronary condition is very serious. If you don't reduce the stress in his life, *he will die.* So, when he gets up in the morning, make his favorite breakfast and bring it to him in bed. Give him a hug and a kiss as he goes out the door. Call him at work to say he's a great provider and you appreciate him. When he gets home, have a delicious dinner waiting for him. If he wants something special in the bedroom, give it to him. Above all, *always be sweet to him.* You stick to that; Max could live another twenty years."

Mrs. Goldberg nods quietly and leaves the office.

She gets in the car beside a worried Max.

"What did the doctor say?"

"He said you're not going to make it."

#15

BEFORE YOU I AM NOTHING

During Yom Kippur services, the rabbi raises his arms to the heavens and cries out, "Oh God, before you I am nothing!"

Seeing this, the cantor beats his chest and shouts, "Oh God, before you I am nothing!"

Inspired by their piety, a humble baker in the back of the congregation stands and proclaims, "Oh God, before you I am nothing!"

The rabbi turns to the cantor and says, "Hmph, look who thinks he's nothing."

#16

THE SECOND WIFE

Morty Greenbaum shows up at the country club with his new wife, a gorgeous woman half his age.

His buddies are impressed.

"Morty, how'd get you get a hottie like her to marry you?!"

"I lied about my age."

"You told her you're 50?"

"No, I told her I'm 90."

#17

THE POKER GAME

A rabbi, a priest, and a minister are playing poker when cops raid the game.

The lead officer asks the priest, "Father Murphy, were you gambling?"

Father Murphy silently asks God to forgive him for what he is about to say.

"No, officer. I was not gambling."

"Pastor Johnson, were you gambling?"

Pastor Johnson makes the same silent appeal to Heaven.

"No, officer. I was not gambling."

"Rabbi Goldstein, were you gambling?"

"Gambling . . . ?" he asks, glancing at the priest and the minister, " . . . with who?"

#18

BACK IN THE U.S.S.R.

During the dark years of Soviet Russia, Yitzy brings his shoes in for a repair.

The shoemaker says, "They'll be ready in ten years."

"Ten years from today?"

"Correct."

"That's no good. I've got the plumber coming."

#19

THE INTERFAITH CONFERENCE

At an interfaith conference, a priest, a minister, and a rabbi sit on a panel.

The moderator asks, "What do you hope people will say about you at your funeral?"

The priest says, "At my funeral, I hope they'll say I put the needs of my congregation before my own."

The minister says, "At my funeral, I hope they'll say I extended my ministry beyond the walls of my church."

The rabbi says, "At my funeral, I hope they'll say, 'Look, he's moving!'"

#20

THREE BROTHERS, THREE BEERS

Fleeing the pogroms in Russia, brothers Abe, Solly, and Moshe end up in three different corners of the world: Abe in New York, Solly in London, and Moshe in Melbourne.

They agree to stay close by drinking a beer for each other every week.

And that's why Solly goes to the same London pub every Monday night, orders three beers, and sits in the corner, thinking of his brothers.

The regulars get to know him, and they understand why he orders three beers on the same day every week.

Many years go by until one Monday night, Solly comes into the pub and orders two beers.

The regulars look at each other, concerned. Finally, the bartender walks over to Solly.

"We noticed you only ordered two beers, Solly. Did something . . . happen to one of your brothers?"

"No, not at all. I just decided to quit drinking."

#21

THE GREAT DEBATE

Four rabbis engage in heated debate about a Torah law. After everyone makes their case, they vote and it's three to one against Rabbi Eliezer.

But Rabbi Eliezer is sure they're wrong. He cries out to Heaven, "God, please send a sign to prove that I am right!"

Out of a clear blue sky, it begins to snow. Rabbi Eliezer says, "You see?!"

One of the rabbis says, "So, it's snowing in winter. This is a sign?"

Rabbi Eliezer implores, "God, please make it clearer to them!"

A massive icicle falls from the sky and splits a tree in half. Rabbi Eliezer says, "A miracle!"

The second rabbi says, "An icicle from the sky? This you call a miracle?"

Before Eliezer can open his mouth, the sky darkens and a booming voice calls out from Heaven, "THE LAW IS ACCORDING TO RABBI ELIEZER!"

"There! Now you can't deny it!"

And the third rabbi says, "Meh. So now it's three to two."

#22

BLIND MAN ON PASSOVER

A blind man is sitting on a park bench when a rabbi sits down next to him.

It's Passover, and the rabbi takes out a piece of matzah for a snack.

Feeling friendly, he offers a piece of the perforated flat-bread to his sightless neighbor.

After a moment, the blind man turns to the rabbi and says, "Who wrote this garbage?"

#23

THE RABBI AND THE CABBIE

A rabbi and a Tel Aviv cab driver wait in line to enter Heaven.

The rabbi looks confident, the cabbie seems nervous. When they reach Heaven's gate, both get in and the cabbie breathes a sigh of relief.

They part company, and the rabbi is taken to his home for eternity: a spacious apartment in a charming building on a nice street.

He's enjoying the view from his balcony when he notices the cabbie from Tel Aviv receiving his eternal residence on a hilltop nearby, a sprawling mansion with acres of grass.

The rabbi calls Heaven's gate.

"I don't mean to complain, and my apartment *is* very nice, but I dedicated my *entire life* to bringing my congregants closer to the Lord. And I noticed that the cabbie from Tel Aviv got a hilltop mansion . . . ?"

"Rabbi, when you were sermonizing, a lot of people were sleeping. When that cabbie was driving, everybody was praying!"

#24

THE NEW SON-IN-LAW

A businessman's daughter marries a young Torah scholar.

The businessman calls in his new son-in-law for a meeting.

"My boy, I love my daughter. That's why I've decided to make you a partner in my business. All you have to do is come into the factory every day and learn the ropes."

"Factory? That's very noisy. I can't work in a factory."

"OK, so we'll put you in the office and you'll take over some of the admin."

"Office? No, no I really can't sit behind a desk all day."

"Son, I just made you a partner in a successful business, but you can't work in the factory because it's too noisy and you can't work in the office because you can't sit behind a desk? What am I supposed to do with you?"

"Oh, that's easy. Buy me out."

#25

THE MOM AND THE SHRINK

A guy goes to see his psychiatrist.

"Doctor, I had the weirdest dream. I was talking to my mother, but she had your face! I was so freaked out, I couldn't get back to sleep. I tossed and turned all night. Finally, I got up at 7 a.m., grabbed some coffee and a donut, and rushed over here. Doctor, what do you think the dream means?"

The doctor studies him for a moment. Then she says, "Coffee and a donut? This you call breakfast?"

#26

SPEED GOLF

A rabbi, a priest, and an imam have been playing golf together for years. They like to play early, and they like to play fast.

One day, they find themselves behind a twosome who are extremely slow. On every hole the guys wait and watch while the players in front of them talk over every shot.

When the clergymen finally get off the course, they approach the starter[11] in a huff.

"That twosome ahead of us was ridiculous! Don't ever stick us behind them again. In fact, they should be banned!"

"I'm sorry, but that was a blind golfer and his aide."

"Oh," says the imam. "I feel terrible. I'm going to pray for inspiration on how I can be of service to blind people."

The priest says, "I'm going to talk to my church about this. We're going to take up a collection for the blind golfer's association."

The rabbi says, "Couldn't they play at night?"

---

11 The person charged with getting the groups started on time.

#27

BABY BLESSING

A couple goes to see a visiting rabbi for a blessing because they've been trying without success to have a baby.

"You caught me at the right time. I'm on my way to Israel. Write down your names and I'll insert them in a prayer for children. I'll place the note in the Western Wall in Jerusalem."

Five years later, the rabbi is back in town, and he runs into the woman.

"Nu? Did you have children? Was your prayer answered?"

"Yes, Rabbi, we have eleven children."

"Eleven kids in five years?!"

"Yes, Rabbi. The first year we had twins. The second year we had twins. Then we had one. Then we had triplets. And then we had triplets again."

"Incredible! Where's your husband?"

"He's actually in Israel right now."

"Really? Is he there on business?"

"No, he's at the Western Wall, looking for that note."

#28

WIVES AND GOLF

Moshe, Avi, and Yitzy are walking up the fairway. One of them is grumbling.

"What's the matter, Moshe?"

"You know what I had to do so I could come out and play golf with you guys? I had to reorganize the whole garage and build shelves. It took forever."

Avi says, "What are you complaining about? I had to build my wife a whole new kitchen."

Yitzy says, "Amateurs. This morning at 5:30 a.m., my big alarm clock with the two bells went BRRRRRNNNNNGGGGGG!! I elbowed the wife and said 'Honey, golf course or intercourse?' She said, 'Don't forget your sweater.'"

#29

THE SERMON

After services one Shabbos, the rabbi is approached by Larry Levy, the famous TV producer.

"Rabbi Cohen, that sermon was amazing. In fact, I want to put you on my talk show on national TV."

"Oh my. I'm flattered. That would be wonderful!"

"Just one thing, Rabbi. TV attention span is much shorter. You can't do a 25-minute sermon."

"I see. Well, I could cut the opening anecdote about my trip to Brazil. That would chop it down to 18 or 19 minutes."

"Yeah, Rabbi, that's still too long."

"Instead of five examples of the teaching, I could do it with three. That would make it 12 minutes."

"Now we're cookin' Rabbi, but it's got to be shorter than that."

"Well, really I just need one strong example. Beginning, middle, end, and a nice takeaway. If I take that route, I could do the whole sermon in five minutes flat."

"Ah. So, Rabbi, why didn't you?"

#30

THE CONVERSION SPECIAL

Two Jews, Benny and Mayshe, are walking down the street when they pass a church with a big sign in front.

We'll Pay You $1000 to Convert!

Mayshe goes inside and walks out ten minutes later.

Benny says, "Did they really give you a thousand dollars?"

"Is that all you people think about, the money?"

#31

THE FUNERAL DIRECTOR

A lady calls the Mount Sinai Funeral Home.

"Hello, this is Marcia Goldberg. My husband passed away this morning. Please come and pick him up."

"But, Mrs. Goldberg, we buried your husband last year."

"Yes, I remarried."

"Oh, mazel tov!"

#32

THE BUILDING CAMPAIGN

A rabbi and a minister become friends, meeting every year and often talking shop at an interfaith conference

"Rabbi, you're so good at fundraising. I'm having trouble at my church. Donations are way down."

"Do you have a building fund?"

"No."

"My friend, you *gotta* have a building fund! Then people will donate."

The following year, they meet again.

"Rabbi, you were right! Donations for the building fund are pouring in. It's fantastic! Thank you so much."

Another year goes by.

"Well, it was good while it lasted, but we finished the building and now donations are way down."

"You finished the building? Who told you to finish the building? You never finish the building!"

#33

YITZY'S RANCH

Three men are sitting next to each other on a plane flying out of Texas: two big guys with cowboy hats and a little old Jew.[12]

They get to talking and one of the big fellas says, "I own a place. Thousand acres, thousand head of cattle. My name's Keith and I call it Circle K."

"I own a place, too. Ten thousand acres. Ten thousand head of cattle. Name's John, and I call it Big John's."

"That's very nice, gentlemen. I only own a hundred acres, no cattle. My name is Yitzy."

"That's OK, Yitzy. What do you call your place?"

"Downtown Dallas."

---

12 If your audience is *frum*, which is to say Orthodox, all these jokes work better with "Yid" in place of "Jew." Sadly, too many Jews (Yidden) have come to believe that "Yid" is an insult. It is not. It's what we call ourselves in Yiddish, and it's an appellation in which we can take great pride.

#34

THE CHINESE RESTAURANT

A rabbi is walking down the street during Passover when he sees the shul president up ahead. The rabbi hustles forward to discuss some business, but before he can catch up, the president enters a non-kosher Chinese restaurant.

The rabbi can't believe his eyes. He watches through the window of the restaurant as the shul president gets a plate of beef lo mein from the buffet and starts to eat.

Unable to contain himself any longer, the rabbi barges in.

"Shimon, what are you doing? I saw you eating that non-kosher food! And during Passover to boot?!"

"Rabbi, did you see me enter this restaurant?"

"Yes!"

"Did you see me pick up the food?"

"Yes!"

"Did you see me eat the food?"

"Yes!"

"Well, then, what's the problem? It was all done under rabbinical supervision."

#35

THE FIANCÉ

A newly engaged woman brings her fiancé home to meet her parents. After dinner, her mother suggests the gentlemen go outside for a cigar.

"So, young man, what are your plans for the future?"

"I'm a Torah scholar."

"Wonderful, but what will you do to pay the rent?"

"I'll study, and God will provide."

"Yes, but eventually you need to buy a nice house for my daughter to live in. Like the one she grew up in."

"I'll concentrate on my studies, and God will provide."

"What about children? How will you support them? And how will you pay for their education?"

"Don't worry, sir. God will provide."

Later that night, the wife asks her husband, "How'd it go, honey?"

"Well, the kid has no job and no prospects. But on the plus side, he thinks I'm God."

#36

THE FLOOD

It's been raining for days. Flood waters are rising. Ari stands on his porch, praying that the rain will stop.

His neighbor approaches in a rowboat.

"Ari! We're evacuating everyone! Get in the boat!"

"Don't worry about me, God will save me!"

The waters keep rising and Ari is now on the second floor of his house.

Someone comes by in a motorboat.

"Ari, get in the boat!"

"It's OK, God will save me!"

The flood keeps rising and Ari's praying on the roof. A helicopter hovers overhead with a rope ladder and a PA system.

"Grab the ladder! Climb into the helicopter!"

"No need! God will save me!"

The waters rise some more, and Ari finally drowns.

When he arrives in Heaven, he says, "God, I was such a faithful Yid. I kept praying You would save me! Why didn't you?"

"Ari, I sent you two boats and a helicopter. What more did you want?"[13]

---

13 This joke works beautifully as a parable about seeing God's hand in everything, and being that hand when it's time to help others.

#37

GOLDBERG'S SLED

Moskowitz is lying in bed at night, unable to sleep, his mind racing . . .

Everything happens to me, I finally get my house set up the way I like it and the landlord says I gotta move out. I finally find a new place and they tell me I gotta move in tomorrow or they're giving it to someone else. And tonight of all nights there's a blizzard! How am I going to move all my stuff in the snow?! . . . Wait a minute, Goldberg down the street has a sled! I can borrow Goldberg's sled. . . . But what if Goldberg won't lend me his sled? . . . Not lend me his sled?? I've been such a good neighbor to him! I say hello every morning! I even lent him my lawnmower! Of course he's going to lend me his sled! . . . Yeah, but people are funny. What if he won't lend me the sled? . . . What a rat! In my hour of need, he's not going to lend me his sled?! . . . When my life is basically over unless he lends it, he's gonna say no?! Who does he think he is?!

Moskowitz gets so worked up, he throws on his boots, trudges through the snow, and bangs on Goldberg's door at 2 a.m.

Goldberg finally opens it and rubbing his eyes says, "What's going on?"

And Moskowitz, red in the face, yells back, "Goldberg, you can keep your stinkin' sled!"

#38

THE BIG WAVE

Rivkah Silverman is walking on the beach with her little grandson.

Suddenly a huge wave sweeps the boy out to sea.

Desperate, Rivkah looks up to Heaven and says, "God, please rescue my grandson! My only grandson, the light of my life!"

Miraculously, the next big wave deposits the little boy at her feet, unharmed.

Rivkah looks up to heaven and says, "He had a hat."[14]

---

14 This may not be the greatest Jewish joke of all time, but it's a candidate for the most Jewish joke of all time.

#39

THE LOTTERY

Zack is going through a rough period. His business isn't doing well, he's got a bunch of kids to feed, and his wife is pressuring him.

Every morning, he goes to shul and prays, "Please, God, let me win the lottery. Nothing else could fix my life like winning the lottery."

Morning after morning after morning he prays.

"Please, God, let me win the lottery!"

Until one day, in the middle of his prayers, he hears a voice from Heaven.

"Zack, meet me halfway. Buy a ticket!"

#40

HAM SANDWICH

A priest and a rabbi sit next to each other on a long plane ride, and they're having a great time chatting.

Toward the end of the flight, the priest says, "Tell me, Rabbi, did you ever in all your years succumb to temptation and try a little ham?"

"You know what, Father? I'll confess. I was so curious about it, that one time I did have a ham sandwich."

The priest nods.

"Father, now that we're friends, let me ask you something. In all your years, did you ever succumb to temptation and see what it was like to be with a woman?"

"Yes, Rabbi, I confess it. One time I gave in and experienced the joys of the flesh."

The rabbi nods.

"So, Father, beats the heck out of a ham sandwich, huh?"

#41

THE NEW SHARON

Sharon has a heart attack and gets rushed to the hospital. She arrives with no pulse, and her soul departs from her body.

Sharon appears before God and asks, "God, is that it?"

"No, Sharon, you have another thirty years to go. Enjoy your life."

Back in the emergency room, the electric shocks work and Sharon regains consciousness. Overjoyed with her new lease on life, she decides to make the most of it. And since she's in the hospital anyway, she orders a tummy tuck, liposuction, and breast augmentation. She also brings in a hairdresser, a beautician, and a stylist to complete the makeover.

When she leaves the hospital, Sharon looks spectacular.

She steps into the street, gets run over by an ambulance and is killed instantly.

Her soul returns to heaven and again she comes before God.

"God, what happened? You said I had another thirty years. Why didn't you save me?"

"Sharon, is that you? I didn't recognize you!"

#42

THE OLD MAN CONFESSES

An old man enters a church and goes to confession.

"Forgive me, Father, for I have sinned. I'm eighty years old and earlier this week I was walking home from the library when a car pulled up with two young ladies in it. They said they were on spring break and asked for directions. We got to talking and they offered me a ride home. On the way, they asked me how old I am. When I told them, they said 'When's the last time you had sex?' I said it's been years. They said, 'Would you like to have a good time?' I said sure, so they came up to my apartment and for the next two nights and the day in between, hoo wee! They're still there and they said when I get home, we're gonna do something I never imagined in my wildest dreams. So that's my confession."

"I see. Tell me, how long has it been since your last confession?"

"Oh, this is my first time, Father."

"You're eighty years old and you've never made confession before?"

"No, I'm Jewish."

"Well, in that case, why are you telling me all this?"

"Father, I'm telling everybody!"

#43

JEWISH TELEGRAM

What's a Jewish telegram?[15]

START WORRYING.

DETAILS TO FOLLOW.

---

15 Long before email, and even before telephones, if you wanted to send a message quickly you sent a telegram via a company like Western Union. And you paid by the word.

#44

THE YOM KIPPUR TICKET

A man shows up at synagogue on Yom Kippur without a ticket and the usher won't let him in.

"I'm not staying, I just need to ask my friend a question."

"OK, but no praying!"

#45

DESERT ISLAND

A religious Jew is shipwrecked and spends thirty years on a deserted island. Finally, a passing ship sees his bonfire and sends a rescue party.

Curious how he spent thirty years living alone, the ship's captain comes ashore and gets a tour of the island. He sees the hut, the tools, the cooking utensils, etc.

"But what did you do for thirty years so you wouldn't go insane being all alone?"

"I'll show you."

They walk through the jungle and come to a clearing where there's a magnificent synagogue, like a European cathedral.

"Oh, I see. It must've taken you thirty years build that by hand."

"Fifteen, actually. I'll show you what I did for the next fifteen."

They walk through the jungle to another clearing and find another magnificent synagogue.

"I understand the need to keep busy, but why two synagogues?"

"The first one I pray in every day. The second one? I would never set foot in that place!"

#46

THE PLANE RIDE

On El Al 5 from LA to Tel Aviv, Yitzy is settling in for the night, hoping to get some sleep before his big meeting in Israel.

He puts on his sleep mask and is trying to relax when the man sitting next to him lets out a deep sigh.

"Oy, am I thirsty! Oy! Am I thirsty!"

Yitzy wonders, *Is this gonna go on all night?*

"Oy! Am I thirsty."

It is.

"Oy yoy yoy, am I thirsty!"

Yitzy is getting annoyed. He summons a flight attendant, asks for a cup of water and gives it to the man next to him. The man drinks it all, and hands Yitzy the cup.

Yitzy stuffs it into the seat back, pulls down his sleep mask, and reclines his chair.

A minute later . . .

"Oy! Was I thirsty!"

#47

MARTIN WATERS III

Back when Jews were restricted from the New York Athletic Club, Milton Wasserstein was desperate to become a member.

He changed his name to Martin Waters III and underwent surgery to minimize his nose.

He spent a year in England, working with a tutor to lose his accent.

Upon returning, he spent another year getting to know members of the club.

Finally, it was time to appear before the membership committee.

The chairman asked, "What is your name?"

"Martin Waters III."

"Are you married, Mr. Waters?"

"Yes, I am. Penelope and I have three lovely children. Babs is our youngest, Hunter is the middle child, and Martin Waters IV is our eldest."

"Education?"

"The usual—Eton, Oxford. Young Martin is there now."

"Very good. And your religious affiliation?"

"We're Goyim[16] of course."

---

16 Lit. nations, i.e. non-Jews. God commands the Jews to be an *ohr la-goyim*, a light unto the nations (Isaiah 42:6).

#48

SAUL'S FINAL WISH

Old Saul Mankewitz is lying on his deathbed surrounded by his family. The smell of baking apple cake wafts into the room.

His eyes flutter open.

In a whisper he croaks, "Is that my Sarah's apple cake? Bring me a piece, so it can be the last thing I taste in this world."

His grandson runs out of the room, and returns a moment later, emptyhanded.

"Bubbe says she's saving it for the shiva."

#49

NEW GUY AT THE POOL

At a retirement community in Florida, Sadie spots a new male resident relaxing by the pool. She touches up her lipstick and approaches.

"Excuse me, is this seat taken?"

"Be my guest."

Sadie sits beside him. "So, what's your name?"

"Howie."

"And where are you from, Howie?"

"Cleveland."

"I have a cousin in Cleveland! What did you do there?"

"I was in prison."

"Prison! And may I ask what for?"

"I was married to a woman who wouldn't stop hounding me with questions. One day I finally snapped and killed her with a knife, cut her up with a saw, and fed her to wild boars. For this I spent thirty-five years in prison."

Sadie's eyes widen. "I see . . . So, you're single?"

#50

A PIECE OF CAKE

Yossy and Mendy are sitting at a table together and there are two pieces of cake left, a big one and a little one. They sit there for a while and finally Yossy takes the bigger piece of cake.

Mendy says, "That wasn't very generous of you."

"Why, which one would you have taken?"

"I would have taken the smaller one, of course."

"Well then, you got it!"

#51

WRONG WAY DRIVER

An eighty-five-year-old woman is driving down the freeway when her phone rings. It's her husband.

"Sylvia! Be careful! I heard on the news there's a lunatic driving the wrong direction on the I-5!"

"What do you mean one lunatic? There are hundreds!"

#52

ALL IN GOOD TIME

A boy talks to God while walking through a forest.

"God, what's a million years like for you?"

"My son, for me a million years is like a second."

"God, what is a million dollars to you?"

"My son, a million dollars means nothing to me."

"So, can I have a million dollars?"

"Sure, in a second."

#53

HEIR SEEKS WIFE

Yitzy is a single guy living at home and working in the family business.

When his father becomes deathly ill, Yitzy discovers that he stands to inherit a large fortune. He decides he needs a wife to share it with.

That evening in a restaurant, he notices a beautiful woman across the room. Summoning all his courage, he walks over and introduces himself.

"I may seem like an average guy, but in the near future I stand to inherit 50 million dollars."

Impressed, the woman asks for his business card.

Three weeks later, she becomes his stepmother.

#54

THE BEEF BARLEY SOUP

Every day, Morrie eats lunch in the same deli, and every day he orders the beef barley soup.

One day, he calls the waiter back and says, "Taste the soup."

"What's wrong, Morrie?"

"Taste the soup."

"Is it too salty?"

"Taste the soup."

"Is it cold?"

"Just taste the soup!"

"Fine. Where's the spoon?"

"Aha!"

#55

THE SUCCESSFUL MAN

There's an old saying about marriage.

Behind every successful man, there's a surprised mother-in-law.

#56

A HEALTHY DIET

Abe is an eater, and his favorite foods are pastrami, schmaltz, rugelach, cholent . . . all of which he washes down with black cherry soda.

At Abe's annual physical, the doctor shakes his head.

"Abe, the way you eat, you're killing yourself. Best thing for you to do is give up all those fattening foods."

Abe nods.

"Okay, doc. What's the next best thing?"

#57

A BUMPY FLIGHT

A priest and a rabbi are flying to the Holy Land when the plane experiences heavy turbulence. They struggle to remain calm.

The pilot announces that the engines are failing, and everybody should brace for a water landing. During the ensuing panic, the priest is surprised to see the rabbi make the sign of the cross.

They hit the Atlantic Ocean, and miraculously no one is harmed.

As they wait on a raft to be rescued, the priest turns to the rabbi.

"I noticed you crossed yourself at 20,000 feet. Perhaps it was your conversion that delivered us all from destruction!"

"Well, Father, I too am grateful for our deliverance, but I was just doing my emergency check: spectacles, testicles, wallet, and cigars."

#58

THE NEW YEAR'S EVE PARTY

Barry goes to a New Year's Eve party.

He's having a great time until he realizes he lost his wallet.

Barry's not a shy guy, so he stands up and yells, "Excuse me! Excuse me! I lost my wallet with $500 in it. I'll give $50 to whoever finds it!"

From the back of the room comes a voice, "I'll give $75!"

#59

SHMULY AND THE LAMPPOST

Mendel sees his pal Shmuly crawling around on his hands and knees near a lamp post, looking for something.

"Shmuly, what are you looking for?"

"My car keys."

"You dropped them right here?"

"No, I dropped them down the street."

"So why are you looking here?"

"The light is much better!"[17]

---

17 Give this one some thought. It's a profound lesson on human nature.

#60

A DATE FOR LAZER

Rachel the matchmaker comes to see Lazer the ugly butcher.

"What can I get for you today, Rachel? Maybe a nice brisket?"

"Lazer, today I'm here for you!"

"For me? After all these years, you have a match for me?"

"I do."

"Is she ugly?"

"Take a look at her picture."

"Oh my God, she's beautiful!"

"Not only is she beautiful, Lazer, she's rich! And you are going on a date with her Saturday night!"

"You're telling me, Lazer the ugly butcher, that I'm going out with this beautiful woman, this Saturday night. And she's rich?"

"Yes!"

"Wow. She must be crazy."

"Well, you can't have everything."

#61

DON'T DRINK, DON'T SMOKE

Ben Goldfarb is approached by a homeless guy.

"Mister, can you spare a few bucks so I can buy dinner?"

"Are you gonna use the money to buy whisky?"

"No, I stopped drinking years ago."

"Will you spend it on cigarettes?"

"Mister, I quit way back, when the price shot up."

"Will you spend it on golf?"

"I haven't played golf in twenty years!"

"OK, I'm not going to give you a few bucks. I'm gonna take you home for a terrific dinner, cooked by my wife."

"Really? That'd be awesome, but you sure it's OK? I'm dirty, and I don't smell good."

"Brother, that's alright. I just want my wife to see what a man looks like when he gives up drinking, smoking, and golfing."

#62

HER NEW APARTMENT

Mitzy moves into a new apartment and calls her best friend.

"Come see my new place!"

"I'd love to! Where do you live?"

"780 East 86th. When you get there, open the lobby door with your right elbow, and ring 3A with your left. I'll buzz you in, open the door with your right elbow, press the elevator button with your left, get inside, and press number 3 with your right elbow. Get off on 3 and ring the doorbell on 3A with your left elbow, and I'll scream for joy when I see you!"

"I'm excited to see you too. But Mitzy, what's with all the elbows?"

"What, you're coming empty-handed?"

#63

SELLING TIES TO THE TALIBAN

A fleeing Taliban terrorist, desperate for water, is trudging through the desert when he sees something in the distance.

Praying it isn't a mirage, he hurries toward the object only to find a little old Jew selling ties from a rack.

The terrorist blurts, "Give me water!"

"Sorry, no water. Would you like to buy a tie? They're only $5."

"Infidel! I don't need a western adornment. I spit on your ties! I need water!"

"Sorry, no water, just ties. Pure silk, and only $5."

"A curse on your ties! I'd twist one around your neck and choke you but . . . I need my strength to find water!"

"Nu, so you don't want to buy a tie from me, and you hate me, you call me infidel and threaten my life. But I fear only God, so I will tell you that if you go west, over that hill for about two miles, you'll find a restaurant. They serve fine food and all the ice-cold water you can drink. Go in peace."

Grumbling another curse, the desperate terrorist staggers west, over the hill.

Hours later, he crawls back, nearly dead, and gasps, "They wouldn't let me in without a tie!"

#64

SHE WAS ALWAYS BY HIS SIDE

Evan Cohen lies on his death bed. He turns to his wife.

"Lisa, you've always been by my side."

"Yes, dear."

"When I broke my leg at twenty-five, you were by my side."

"I was."

"When I had my heart attack at forty-five, you were by my side."

"I remember."

"When I had my second heart attack at sixty-five, you were by my side. When I broke my hip at seventy-five, you were by my side. And now when I'm dying, you're at my side. Lisa . . ."

"Yes, darling?"

" . . . you're a jinx!!"

#65

PULLED OVER FOR SPEEDING

A little old Jewish lady gets pulled over for speeding.

"Is there a problem, officer?"

"Yes, ma'am, you were speeding. Can I see your license please?"

"I'd give it to you, but I lost it for drunk driving."

"I see. Vehicle registration please."

"Can't do that either. This car is stolen."

"You stole it?"

"Yes, and I killed the owner."

"You what?"

"Killed him. Dismembered him. His body parts are in the trunk."

The officer calls for back-up. Within minutes, six police cars circle the little old Jewish lady's car.

A senior officer slowly approaches with his hand on his gun.

"Ma'am, step out of your vehicle please!"

She steps out of her vehicle. "Is there a problem, sir?"

"My patrol officer said you stole this car and murdered its owner."

"Stole the car and murdered the owner?!"

"Yes. Open the trunk, please."

She does. It's empty.

"Is this your car, ma'am?"

"Yes, here's the registration."

"My patrol officer said you lost your license?"

"No, here it is."

The senior officer examines her license. "Sorry for the misunderstanding, ma'am. For some reason, my patrol officer reported that you lost your license for DUI, stole this car, and that you murdered and dismembered its owner."

"He must be insane. I wouldn't be surprised if he told you I was speeding, too."

#66

THE PRETZEL LADY

An old lady sells pretzels on a street corner for twenty-five cents. Every day, a young businessman passes her pretzel stand around lunchtime and leaves her a quarter without taking a pretzel.

This goes on for three years, without a word passing between them.

One day, the young businessman leaves his quarter as usual, and the pretzel lady speaks up for the first time.

"Sir, I appreciate your business, but I must tell you the price went up. My pretzels are now thirty-five cents!"

#67

HER NEW SON-IN-LAW

We're back in Poland when marriages were arranged. Yankel and Moishe are riding a train, thinking about their brides—whom they're about to meet for the first time.

Suddenly, Yankel jumps up and says, "I'm not ready for marriage. I'm not getting married!" He grabs his suitcase and runs off the train at the next stop. Moishe watches him go.

A day later he reaches his destination, where the two mothers of the prospective brides are shocked to discover there's only one groom on the train.

"He's mine!"

"Not on your life! He'll marry *my* daughter!"

Moishe suggests they all go to the rabbi for a ruling.

"We learn the solution from King Solomon: cut the boy in two, and each of you take half."

The first mother looks shocked.

The second mother says, "Fine! Cut him in two!"

Says the rabbi, "That's the real mother-in-law!"[18]

---

18 See I Kings 3:16-28, the famous story of King Solomon and the disputed baby.

#68

DIRECTIONS IN THE OLD CITY

A Jewish American tourist wandering through the Old City of Jerusalem approaches a native.

"Excuse me, how long will it take me to walk to the Western Wall?"

The Israeli stares at him.

"I said how long will it take me to get to the Wall from here?"

No answer.

The American asks again in Hebrew, but the Israeli still doesn't respond.

The American walks away.

The Israeli runs up behind him and says, "It'll take you seven minutes from here!"

"Why didn't you say so before?"

"I didn't know how fast you walk."

#69

THE DOCTOR & THE LAWYER

A lawyer and a doctor meet in synagogue on Shabbos.

The doctor says, "You don't know how lucky you are. Every time I come here to pray, people hound me with their medical problems. This one has stomach trouble. That one has back pain. Everybody wants free advice. But you? Nobody bothers you with legal questions. How do you do it?"

The lawyer responds, "Nothing to it. Any time somebody asks me for legal advice, I send them a bill on Monday."

The doctor loves the idea. Come Monday, he's sitting in his office writing up a bunch of bills when there's a knock on his door.

It's the mailman, with a bill from the lawyer.

#70

THE DOCTOR OF CHELM

A new doctor opens his office in Chelm[19] and his first patient is the Great Sage of Chelm, Rabbi Chernowitz.

"Doctor, I hurt all over."

"All over where?"

"Everywhere! When I touch my leg—ouch!—it hurts. When I touch my arm—ouch!—it hurts. When I touch my head—ouch!—it hurts. When I touch my chest—ouch!—it really hurts."

"Rabbi, I know for a fact that your body is fine."

"How could you possibly know that, Doctor?"

"Because your finger is broken."

---

19 In the annals of Jewish humor, the town of Chelm is widely known for its IQ-challenged residents.

#71

THE HAIRCUT

Rabbi Schwartzman is delivering his biggest sermon of the year. In the middle of the speech, Yankel gets up and walks out of the synagogue.

The next day, Rabbi Schwartzman sees Yankel on the street.

"Yankel, wait a second!"

"Hello, Rabbi."

"Why did you walk out during my sermon yesterday?"

"I needed a haircut."

"You couldn't get your hair cut before my sermon?"

"I didn't need it then."

#72

LATE FOR HEBREW SCHOOL

"Abe, wake up, you'll be late for Hebrew School!"

"No, Mom, I don't wanna go."

"Why don't you want to go?"

"Because the teachers hate me and all the kids make fun of me."

"Too bad. You still have to attend."

"Give me one good reason why I should."

"I'll give you two! You're fifty-six years old and you're the rabbi!"

#73

THE COUPLE THAT NEVER FOUGHT

Back in the days when millions of Jews lived in the villages of Poland and Ukraine, a young Torah scholar was soon to be wed.

He heard about an old couple who never had a fight in sixty years of marriage. Eager to learn their secret, he walked for days to hear the husband's story:

The day after we married, I went to my in-laws' house with a donkey-cart and loaded all my wife's possessions into it. We set out for our new home.

After a couple hours of walking, the donkey suddenly stopped. My wife walked around in front of the donkey, looked him in the eye and said, "That's one."

An hour later, the donkey took another unauthorized break. My wife said, "That's two."

An hour after that, the donkey stopped again and wouldn't budge. My wife walked around in front of the donkey and said, "That's three." Then she pulled out a gun and shot the donkey dead.

I said to her, "Don't you think that's a little excessive?"

She said, "That's one."

#74

THE KOSHER DELI

When triplets Abe, Sam, and Moshe turned forty, they discussed where to meet for their birthday lunch. They decided to meet at the kosher deli uptown because it had the best-looking waitresses.

When they turned fifty, they decided to meet at the kosher deli uptown because it had the best pastrami.

When they turned sixty, they decided to meet at the kosher deli uptown because it had the best parking.

When they turned seventy, they decided to meet at the kosher deli uptown because it had a wheelchair accessible bathroom.

When they turned eighty, they decided to meet at the kosher deli uptown because they'd never been there before.

#75

THE JEWISH OPTIMIST

What's the difference between a Jewish pessimist and a Jewish optimist?

The Jewish pessimist says, "Things can't possibly get any worse."

The Jewish optimist says, "Sure they can."

#76

FISH HEADS MAKE YOU SMARTER

Shimmy asked Max, "How did you get so smart? You always make the witty remark."

"The truth is, it's the fish heads I sell in my store. I make a soup out of them, and it speeds up my brain."

"Really? How much do you sell the fish heads for?"

"Ten bucks a pound."

"Give me five pounds."

A week later, Shimmy walks into Max's fish shop.

"You liar! You cheat! Fish heads are scrap—that's why they sell for fifty cents a pound. And you unloaded them on me for fifty bucks!"

"See? You're getting smarter already."

#77

JOSH & THE BIKER

Josh sits at the bar, staring into his bourbon when a large biker with a swastika tattoo on his forehead grabs his drink and downs it.

"Thanks for the drink, Jew-boy."

Josh bursts into tears.

"Come on, Jew-boy, I didn't think you'd cry about it. What's the matter with you?"

"This is the worst day of my life."

"Yeah? You saw a dollar and someone else picked it up?"

"My boss fired me and on the way home I got into an accident and totaled my car. I still owe the loan and my credit cards are maxed out. I took the bus home and found my wife in bed with my best friend. So I came here to work up the courage to end it all. I bought a bourbon, dropped the cyanide into it, and I was watching the poison dissolve when you showed up, and drank the whole thing. But enough about me. How's your day going?"

#78

THE PICKLE MAN

A man walks into a deli on the Lower East Side of New York City and asks the owner, "Do you have pickles?"

"Do I have pickles?! Right here I have sour, half-sour, and oversize. Step over here for the gherkins. This barrel is full of bread and butter pickles. That one's got brine pickles. Those three barrels are all classic dill. That vat holds the sweet dill. And those shelves are for Hungarian, German, and Polish pickles."

"Wow! You must sell a lot of pickles!"

"Well, to be honest, not so many. But the guy I buy from? He can sell pickles!"

#79

HOW A TALMUDIST THINKS

After months of waiting, a talmudist from Leningrad finally receives permission to visit Moscow.

He boards his train and finds himself sitting next to another young man. The talmudist studies him and thinks:

This fellow doesn't look like a farm worker, so he probably comes from this district, and this being a Jewish district, he's probably a Jew.

But if he is a Jew, where could he be going? I'm the only Jew in our district with permission to travel to Moscow.

Ah! Just outside Moscow there's a village called Lesnaya, and Jews don't need special permission to go to Lesnaya. But why would he travel to Lesnaya? Must be he's going to visit one of the Jewish families there. But how many Jewish families are there in Lesnaya? Only two, Davidovich and Orovich. But since the Oroviches are a terrible family, this nice-looking fellow must be visiting the Davidoviches.

The Davidoviches have two children—daughters—so maybe he's their son-in-law. But if he is, then which daughter did he marry? They say Suri Davidovich married a nice lawyer from Budapest, and Esti married a baker from Vinograd. Judging by the expensive coat, this must be Suri's husband. Which means his name is Joseph Cohen.

But if he came from Budapest, with all the antisemitism they have there, he must have changed his name.

What's the Hungarian equivalent of Cohen? Kovacs. But since they allowed him to change his name, he must have special status to change it. What could it be? Must be a doctorate from the university. Nothing less would suffice.

The talmudist turns to his neighbor and says, "Excuse me. Do you mind if I open the window, Dr. Kovacs?"

"Not at all. But how did you know my name?"

"Oh, it was obvious."

#80

THE LAND OF OPPORTUNITY

Three Jewish men fleeing the pogroms in eastern Europe become friends on the ship to America. They agree to reunite in twenty years to see how they all fared in the land of opportunity. Two decades later, they meet again.

Silverman says, "When I arrived, I had no idea how I'd make a living. So, I looked up Silvermans in the phone book and found a distant relative. He was in the silver business and he took me on. After a few years, I married his daughter and became a partner. Now I have a house in the city and another in the mountains. How about you, Goldstein?"

"Believe it or not, same story. I found a relative in the gold business, worked hard, married his daughter and became a partner. Today I live on the top floor of a building that I own, and my grandchildren don't worry how they'll pay for college. How about you, Taylor?"

"I too had no idea how I'd make a living. Despite my name, I never trained as a tailor and it sounded like a lot of work for not a lot of money. So, I went to shul and prayed. I said, 'God, if you make me a prosperous man, I promise to make You my partner.'"

"Nu? So, what happened?"

"What do you mean, what happened? You never heard of Lord & Taylor?

#81

SAGES UNDER THE STARS

Rabbi Karelman, a brilliant talmudist, and his star pupil Yossy are traveling to Vilna when they stop for the night and pitch their tent in an empty field.

Some hours later, Rabbi Karelman wakes up and nudges his student. "Yossy, look up at the sky and tell me what you see."

"I see millions of stars, Rabbi Karelman."

"And from this, what do you deduce?"

"Well, astronomically, this view conveys the vastness of the heavens. Chronometrically, I deduce that the time is approximately a quarter past three. Meteorologically, I suspect that we will have a beautiful day tomorrow. Theologically, I see that God is all powerful, and we occupy a tiny corner of His universe. What do you see, Rabbi Karelman?"

"What I see, Yossy, is that someone stole our tent!"

#82

THE MOST DISCREET PERSON

Six guys are playing poker in their Florida retirement community. Abe loses $500 on a single hand, clutches his chest, and drops dead at the table.

Out of respect to Abe, they play standing up for the next two hours.

When the game finally ends, Meyerowitz looks around and says, "So who's going to tell his wife?"

They cut cards, and Pearlman draws the low hand.

They tell him to be discreet and gentle, don't make the sad situation any worse.

"Discreet? I'm the most discreet person you'll ever meet."

Pearlman goes to Abe's condo at 2 a.m. and knocks. Abe's wife answers through the screen door and asks what he wants.

"Abe lost $500 in a poker game and he's afraid to come home."

"Tell him to drop dead!"

"OK, I'll go tell him."

#83

IF YOU ONLY KNEW

A little old Jewish lady gets on a crowded bus and discovers that she doesn't have the correct change for the fare.

"I'm sorry ma'am but without the correct fare you can't ride."

She places her hand gently on her chest and says, "If you knew what I had, you'd be nicer to me."

He lets her ride. She tries to move down the crowded aisle, but people won't make way for her.

She says, "If you knew what I had, you'd be nicer to me."

The crowd parts like the Red Sea. She reaches the back of the bus and can't find a seat. No one gets up for her.

She says, "If you knew what I had, you'd be nicer to me."

Several people jump up and insist that she take their seat. She settles into a good one by the window.

A passenger leans over to her and says, "I know this is none of my business, but just what is it that you have?"

The little old Jewish lady grins and says, "Chutzpah."

#84

UNDER THE BED

Mitzi's husband Hershel is late coming home again.

Fed up, she writes him a note saying, "I've had it! I've left you. Don't bother coming after me."

Mitzi places the note on his dresser, then hides under the bed to see his reaction.

Hershel finally comes home. She hears him rummage the fridge, walk up the stairs, and enter their bedroom.

She watches him go over to the dresser and pick up her note.

He writes something on the back of it. Then he makes a call.

"She finally left me . . . 'Bout time, right? Darling, from now on, it's you and me. Put on that slinky dress and meet me at the Waldorf. It's gonna be a night to remember and breakfast in bed! . . . I love you too. Can't wait."

Hershel grabs his keys and trots down the stairs. Mitzi hears his car drive off as she emerges from beneath the bed, furious and sobbing.

Wiping her tears, she grabs the paper to see what he wrote.

"I saw your feet. We're out of ice cream. Back in ten minutes."

#85

UNCONVENTIONAL MEDICINE

Mrs. Mandell goes to the doctor's office and sees one of the new young doctors.

Five minutes later, she bursts out of the examination room, screaming as she runs down the corridor.

Gray-haired Dr. Goldberg asks her what's wrong and hears the whole story.

He calms her down, seats her in his office, and asks her to wait there for a moment. Then he hustles over to the young doctor's examination room.

"Are you insane? Mrs. Mandell is sixty-one years old! She has four grown kids and seven grandchildren, and you told her she's pregnant?"

"Does she still have the hiccups?"

#86

A PHONE CALL FROM MOM

Relieved to get a break in her day, Esty jumps to answer the phone.

"Darling, it's your mother. How are you?"

"Oh, Mom, I'm having a bad day. The baby won't stop crying and the dishwasher broke. I haven't gone shopping yet, and I banged my shin so hard I'm limping. The house is a mess and on top of all that, the Geshmans are coming for dinner. I don't know how I'm gonna do it."

"Darling, Mama's got this. Sit down and do absolutely nothing for thirty minutes except relax. I'll do the shopping, clean up your house, and cook dinner. I have a wonderful repairman for the dishwasher, and I'll take the baby for a stroll. So, stop crying, Mama's coming. And I'll even call Moshe to tell him he should come home early and help out for once."

"Moshe? Who's Moshe?"

"Why, Moshe's your husband . . . Is this 564-7721?"

"No, it's 564-7712."

"I'm so sorry! I have the wrong number."

"Oh. Does that mean you're not coming over?"

#87

THE SUPREME LEADER

The Supreme Leader of Iran gets a phone call.

"Mr. Supreme Leader, this is Ori from a little village in Israel. I'm calling to let you know that our morning minyan is officially declaring war on you."

"Well, Ori, this is important news. Tell me, how big is your army?"

"Currently, there is myself, my cousin Ran, our next door neighbor Eitan, and the entire 6 a.m. minyan—that makes eighteen!"

"I must tell you, Ori, that I have one million men in my army ready to move on my command."

"Hmph. I'll call you back."

Next day, Ori calls back.

"All right, Mr. Supreme Leader, the war is still on. We acquired some equipment: two combine harvesters, a bull-dozer, and Eitan's tractor from the farm."

"Ori, I have sixteen thousand tanks and fourteen thousand armored carriers."

"Is that so? I'll call you back."

Next day.

"Shalom, Mr. Supreme Leader, the war is still on. Now we're airborne too! We modified Shimmy's ultra-light with a couple of rifles in the cockpit and the 8 a.m. minyan joined in too."

"Ori, I have bombers and MiG 29 fighter jets, and my bases are surrounded by laser-guided missiles. And since we first spoke, my army has doubled in size to two million men."

"OK, I'll call you back."

Next day.

"Mr. Supreme Leader, I'm sorry to say the war is off."

"I'm very sorry to hear that, Ori. Why the change of heart?"

"We all had a chat, and there's no way we can feed two million prisoners."

#88

SHOE REPAIR

Going through an old drawer, David finds a thirty-year-old ticket for shoe repair. He remembers that he once brought in some shoes for new heels and realizes he must've forgotten all about them.

"I wonder if old Goldberg is still repairing shoes? I haven't been to that neighborhood in ages!"

David drives over, and to his amazement, Goldberg's Shoe Repair is still there, with old Mr. Goldberg working behind the counter. David figures his shoes are long gone, but it can't hurt to ask, so he greets Mr. Goldberg, and shows him the thirty-year-old ticket.

"Any chance the shoes are here?"

"Let me check."

Mr. Goldberg toddles off into the back. A minute later, he calls out, "Got 'em right here!"

"Wow," thinks David, "this guy's a legend."

Mr. Goldberg comes back out, and hands the ticket back to David.

"They'll be ready on Tuesday."

#89

THE PRAYING PARROT

Yankel adopts a pet parrot, hoping it can say a few words. The next morning, he finds the bird rocking back and forth, mumbling.

Yankel listens closely, and he's shocked to hear the parrot praying in Hebrew.

"You're Jewish?!" he says to the bird.

"Yes, and religious too. Rosh Hashanah's coming up. Are we going to shul?"

"You want me to take you to synagogue?! This is unbelievable. Is this some kind of secret? Can I tell my friends about you?"

"Tell anyone you want. Now let me finish davening."[20]

Yankel starts bragging about his Orthodox parrot. No one believes him, so he says, "Ok I'll bet you!"

By Rosh Hashanah he has a thousand dollars in bets riding on the bird. On the Day of Judgement, Yankel walks in with his parrot. Everyone stares. Yankel puts the bird on the podium and urges him to pray.

---

20 Praying.

Nothing. People start chuckling around the room. The parrot clucks a few times and goes silent. Yankel starts to panic.

"Daven!" he whispers to the bird, "like you did at my place!"

Nothing.

When they get back home, Yankel grabs the parrot by its scrawny neck.

"You cost me a thousand bucks, you little twit! How could you do this to me?!"

"Don't be a shmuck, Yankel. Think of the odds we'll get on Yom Kippur!"

#90

WHO SAID MY FATHER DIED?

Yitzy visits the doctor for his annual check-up.

"Yitzy, you're in terrific shape for a sixty-year-old. In fact, you have the body of a guy who's thirty-five. Tell me, how old was your father when he died?"

"Who said my father died?"

"Wow! How old is he?"

"Dad's eighty-two and skis or surfs three times a week."

"Amazing! How old was your grandfather when he died?"

"Who said my grandfather died?"

"You're kidding. Don't tell me he's still active?"

"Grandpa's 102, still skis and surfs, and he's getting married again."

"Why on earth would a 102-year-old want to get married?"

"Who said he wants? His parents made him do it!"

#91

THE MEMORIAL WALL

On Rosh Hashanah the rabbi notices little Sammy staring up at the plaque in the synagogue lobby. It's covered with names, and American flags stand on either side.

The seven-year-old keeps staring at it for some time, so the rabbi walks up and says, "Shana tova, Sammy. May you be inscribed for a good year."

"Shana tova, Rabbi."

The rabbi is about to leave when Sammy asks, "Rabbi, what is this?"

"Well, Sammy, it's a memorial to all the men and women who died in the service."

Silently, they stand together, staring at the large plaque.

Finally Sammy whispers, "Rosh Hashanah or Yom Kippur?"

#92

TELL ME SOMETHING GOOD

Eve and Aaron Rothenberg get ready for bed. Eve stares at her reflection in a full-length mirror.

"All I see in this mirror is an old woman. Wrinkles, bags under my eyes, fat on my legs, flab on my arms. Aaron, tell me something positive so I can feel better about myself."

Aaron considers this for a long moment.

"Well, Eve, there's nothing wrong with your eyesight."

Services for Aaron Rothenberg will be held Tuesday morning at Mt. Sinai Memorial Chapel.

#93

SAM GOES TO CHURCH

Sam goes on a business trip to a new city and can't find a synagogue. He figures God is everywhere, so he enters a church for morning prayers. He takes a seat in the back, puts on his prayer shawl and tefillin, and starts praying silently.

The priest enters, observes the whispering of his congregants and steps up to the front of the room.

"Good morning. I'd like to remind everyone that communion is for Christians."

Sam keeps rocking back and forth, deep in his prayers.

"I repeat, only Christians take communion, so I encourage all others to exit the building."

No response from Sam. Everyone looks to see what the priest will do.

"To be clear, now is the time for Jews to take their leave."

Sam finishes praying, stows his prayer shawl and tefillin in their bags, and walks to the front of the room. He passes the priest without saying a word and approaches the altar, where he picks up a statue of baby Jesus.

"Come bubbeleh, we know where we're not wanted."

#94

THE FATHERLAND

In the 1970s, a Red Army school inspector questions a boy in class.

"Who is your father?"

"The Soviet Union."

"Who is your mother?"

"The Communist Party."

"And what do you want to be when you grow up?"

"I want to be a worker for the glory of the state and the party."

The inspector then points to one of the girls.

"Who is your father?"

"The Soviet Union."

"Who is your mother?"

"The Communist Party."

"And what do you want to be when you grow up?"

"A heroine of the Soviet Union raising many children for the state and the party."

The inspector spots a Jewish boy in the back of the classroom trying to lay low.

"What's your name?"

"Shmuly Rabinovich."

"Who is your father?"

"The Soviet Union."

"Who is your mother?"

"The Communist Party."

"And what do you want to be when you grow up?"

"An orphan."

#95

THE CONCERT HALL

A visitor to Israel attends a performance of the Israeli Philharmonic in the Schechter Concert Hall.

Impressed by its architecture and acoustics, he turns to his neighbor during the intermission and asks, "This is a magnificent auditorium. Was it named after Aryeh Schechter, the great Talmudic scholar?"

"No, it's named after Mike Schechter, the writer."

"Oh? Never heard of him. What did he write?"

"A check."

#96

THAT'S A LOT OF PILLS!

Mrs. Goldberg hasn't been feeling well, so she goes to the doctor. He listens to her extensive list of concerns, performs the examination, and returns with three bottles of pills.

"When you wake up, please take three green pills with a big glass of water. Then take four blue pills with a big glass of water before lunch, and then two more blue pills with a big glass of water after lunch. Then just before going to bed, take five red pills with another big glass of water."

"That's a lot of pills! Doctor, be honest with me. What exactly is my diagnosis?"

"You don't drink enough water."

#97

BUSINESS EXPERIENCE

Diamond runs into his pal Goldberg at the mall.

"Goldberg, it's been months! How's that new business going with Silverman?"

"Well, when we started the company, I provided the money and Silverman provided the business experience. But since then, things have changed."

"Changed how?"

"Now Silverman has the money and I have the business experience."

#98

EINSTEIN'S THEORY OF RELATIVITY

Few people understand what Einstein discovered. Even fewer understood it while he lived.

A crusty old Jew from the old country once asked his grandson, "What's all the fuss about this Einstein?"

"He's the greatest living scientist."

"This I have heard, but what did he invent?"

"The Theory of Relativity."

"And you do what with it?"

"It's pretty complicated, Grandpa."

"It wasn't complicated escaping the Germans? Tell it to me."

"Let me put it this way . . . if a guy sits on a bench with his new girlfriend, an hour feels like a minute. But if the same guy sits on a hot stove, a minute feels like an hour. That's the Theory of Relativity."

"Hmph. And from this Einstein makes a living?"

#99

RABBI, PRIEST, & POLITICIAN

A rabbi, a Hindu priest, and a politician go hiking. Night falls and they're exhausted. The hotel on the map is nowhere to be seen.

They knock on the door of a farm and ask if they can spend the night.

The farmer says, "No problem, but I only have a small room with two beds. One of you will have to sleep in the barn."

The Hindu priest says, "I need no material comforts. I will take the barn."

The rabbi and the politician are settling in when there's a knock on the door. It's the Hindu priest.

"So sorry, my friends, but there is a cow in the barn, and I cannot sleep beside this holy animal."

The rabbi says, "No problem, my brother. I'll take the barn.

The Hindu priest and the politician are settling in when they hear a knock on the door. It's the rabbi.

"So sorry, my friends, but there's a pig in the barn, and I can't sleep beside that filthy animal."

The politician says, "OK, let it be remembered that I sacrificed my comfort for the greater good."

The rabbi and the Hindu priest are settling in when they hear a knock on the door. It's the pig and the cow.

#100

THE AISLE SEAT

Syd is a *yekke*[21] and very particular about air travel. He always asks for a window seat. This time, however, he's given an aisle seat. All his complaints are met with, "Sorry sir, there's nothing we can do."

During the entire flight, he fidgets, squirms, and kvetches. When the plane lands Syd goes straight to customer service.

"I specifically asked for a window seat! I got hit by the drink cart. There was a man snoring across the aisle. A child spilled juice on me. It was miserable! And I specifically asked for a window seat when I purchased the ticket and your airline told me I would get one. But see! Look at my boarding pass. Aisle seat."

"I'm very sorry, sir. Did you by any chance try to trade seats with the person sitting next to you?"

"That was impossible."

"Why, sir?"

"Because there was nobody in that seat!"

---

21 German Jew. Often characterized as a stickler for rules and punctuality.

#101

NAPOLEON'S JEWISH COMMANDER

After winning a major battle, Napoleon summons his commanders to a celebration.

"Gentlemen, today I reward your courage! Ask and it shall be granted!"

The Bavarian commander says, "Autonomy for Bavaria!"

"So, it shall be!"

The Slovakian commander says, "Liberty for Slovakia!"

"So, it shall be!" Napoleon then turns to his Jewish commander.

"And what for you, my loyal friend?"

"I would like please a cup of hot coffee with milk and no sugar, two bagels with cream cheese, and some lox on the side."

"Bring my friend his breakfast immediately!"

As the Jewish commander sits down to eat, his colleagues laugh.

"Fool! Why did you make such a stupid request? You could have asked for your nation's independence!"

"Yes, but what I requested, I got."

#102

THE RICHEST MAN IN TOWN DIES

The richest man in town dies and hundreds of mourners attend the funeral.

Among them, the rabbi notices Yankel, a poor tailor, crying as if his heart is shattered.

"I see how difficult this is for you, Yankel. Were you closely related to the deceased?"

"No," says Yankel, choking back a sob. "I wasn't related at all!"

"But then why are you crying?"

"That's why!"

#103

THE GURU

Judaism is very spiritual. Sadly, however, some Jews don't realize how spiritual our tradition is, and they seek enlightenment elsewhere.

In the 1980s, Mitzy Feingold, an aging lady with a Yiddish accent, calls her travel agent.

"I vont to go to India and see de guru."

"Mitzy, India is crowded, hot, and way too difficult for a lady traveling alone."

"I vont to go to India and see de guru."

"What will you eat? The food is too spicy. You can't drink the water. You'll get typhoid, malaria . . . Why torture yourself?"

"I vont to go to India and see de guru!"

The agent shakes his head and makes the arrangements.

Mitzy arrives in India. Undeterred by the crowds, she makes her way to the ashram.

She joins an enormous line of people waiting to see the guru. Finally, after waiting for hours, she is ushered into the inner sanctum. The great guru sits cross-legged on the floor, with a look of perfect serenity.

Mitzy walks up to the guru, looks him straight in the eye, and says: "Sheldon, come home!"[22]

---

22 This joke arose from the true stories of people like Leonard Cohen, Richard Alpert, Gil Locks, and Allen Ginsberg. Some of them came home when they realized the Judaism they thought they knew was only the shallow end of a much deeper pool, waiting to be explored. If this might be you, I invite you to visit my site accidentaltalmudist.org.

#104

ANTISEMITE WALKS INTO A BAR

An antisemite is drinking in a bar. He notices a Jewish man sitting at a table nearby and doesn't like it.

"Bartender! A round of beer for everyone except the Jew!"

Everyone except the Jew receives a beer.

The antisemite looks over at the Jew with a smug grin.

The Jew smiles back.

The antisemite loses his satisfied expression.

"Bartender! Give everyone a drink of your finest scotch!"

He looks directly at the Jew and adds, "Everyone except the Jew."

Everyone except the Jew receives a glass of premium scotch.

The Jew looks at the antisemite and smiles again.

Furious, the antisemite says to the bartender, "Is that Jew just stupid or pretending to be?"

"Uh no, sir, he's the owner."

#105

THE BUST OF LENIN

An old Jewish man finally gets his visa to leave the USSR and emigrate to Israel. At the Moscow airport, a Red Army guard finds his bust of Lenin.

"What's this?"

"What's this? You mean *who's* this?! This is Comrade Lenin, the genius who created our worker's paradise!"

The Red Army guard chuckles and lets the old man through.

When the old Jew arrives in Tel Aviv, an Israeli customs official finds the bust of Lenin.

"Who's this?"

"Who's this? You mean *what's* this?! This is Lenin, that piece of garbage. I will display him beside my toilet in revenge for all the years he kept me from coming home!"

The Israeli laughs and lets him through.

The old Jew finally joins his family in Jerusalem. While unpacking, his grandson finds the bust of Lenin.

"Grandpa, what's this?"

"Ah, this my child, is eight pounds of gold!"

#106

TWO BURGLARS AND A CHIMNEY

A young man knocks on the door of a great Talmudic scholar.

"Rabbi, I wish to study Talmud."

"Do you know Aramaic?"

"No."

"Hebrew?"

"No."

"Have you ever studied Torah?"

"No, Rabbi, but I graduated from Harvard summa cum laude in philosophy and received a PhD from Yale. I'd like to round out my education with a bit of Talmud."

"I doubt that you are ready for Talmud. It is the broadest and deepest of tomes. If you wish, however, I will examine you in logic, and if you pass the test, I will teach you Talmud."

"Good. I'm well versed in logic."

"First question. Two burglars come down a chimney. One emerges with a clean face, the other with a dirty face. Which one washes his face?"

"The burglar with the dirty face."

"Incorrect. The one with the clean face. Examine the logic. The burglar with a dirty face looks at the one with a clean face and thinks his face is clean. The one with a clean face looks at the burglar with a dirty face and thinks his face is dirty. So, the one with a clean face washes."

"Very clever. Another question please."

"Two burglars come down a chimney. One emerges with a clean face, the other with a dirty face. Which one washes his face?"

"We established that. The burglar with the clean face washes."

"Incorrect. Both wash. Examine the logic. Dirty face thinks his face is clean. Clean face thinks his face is dirty. So, clean face washes. When dirty face sees him washing, however, he realizes his face must be dirty too. Thus, both wash."

"I didn't think of that. Please ask me another."

"Two burglars come down a chimney. One emerges with a clean face, the other with a dirty face. Which one washes his face?"

"Well, we know both wash."

"Incorrect. Neither washes. Examine the logic. Dirty face thinks his face is clean. Clean face thinks his face is dirty. But when clean face sees that dirty face doesn't bother to wash, he also doesn't bother. So neither washes. As you can see, you are not ready for Talmud."

"Rabbi, please, give me one more test."

"Two burglars come down a chimney. One emerges with a clean face, the other with a dirty face. Which one washes his face?"

"Neither!"

"Incorrect. And perhaps now you will see why Harvard and Yale cannot prepare you for Talmud. Tell me, how is it possible that two men come down the same chimney, and one emerges with a clean face, while the other has a dirty face?"

"But you've just given me four contradictory answers to the same question! That's impossible!"

"No, my son, that's the Talmud."

#107

THE BROTHERS & BARON ROTHSCHILD

Two brothers visited the famous Jewish philanthropist Baron Rothschild every month.

They were paupers and each would receive five pounds.

Eventually, one brother died, and the following month the other one came alone.

Rothschild's secretary handed him the usual five pounds.

"What about the other five?"

"Your brother died. This is your five."

"What do you mean?" said the pauper indignantly. "Am I my brother's heir or is Rothschild?!"

#108

THE COMING FLOOD

As a result of climate change, a new flood is predicted by the world's top scientists. They announce it will be cataclysmic, wiping out most of the world's population. And it will happen in thirty days.

To comfort the people of the world, the Pope, the Dalai Lama, and the Chief Rabbi of Israel appear on TV.

The Pope says, "My children, there is still time to accept Jesus as your savior."

The Dalai Lama says, "My friends, we must find inner peace in the midst of this calamity."

The Chief Rabbi says, "My people, we have thirty days to learn how to live underwater!"

#109

THE RABBI'S WATCH

Naughty little Benny steals the rabbi's gold watch.

That night he can't sleep, so the next morning he goes to the rabbi's office before school.

"Rabbi, I stole a gold watch."

"Benny, that's a big sin. Return it to the owner immediately."

"Do you want it?"

"No, I said return it to its owner."

"But he doesn't want it."

"Well, in that case, you can keep it."

#110

LADY, I'M NOT A NICE MAN

Frummy hurries into a pharmacy, gets a prescription filled, and hustles back to the car. Only then does she realize she's locked her keys inside.

"Oh no!"

Not giving up, she looks around for a tool.

"Aha!"

She spots a rusty coat hanger. She tries to open the door but fails.

"I don't know how to do this. God, please, please, please send help!"

A moment later, a scraggly biker pulls up.

"Lady, you need a hand?"

"Yes! My daughter is sick. I have the medicine, but I locked my keys in the car. Can you open it with this hanger?"

"Sure."

Ten seconds later, the car is open.

"Thank You, God, for sending such a nice man!"

"Lady, I'm not a nice man. I got out of prison yesterday. I did three years for car theft."

She beams at the biker.

"And thank You, God, for sending a professional!"

#111

THE MONEY CLIP

A poor Jew finds a money clip with $700 in it. At his synagogue, he reads a notice saying that a wealthy congregant lost his money clip and is offering a $100 reward for it. He spots the owner and gives him the clip.

The rich man counts the money and says, "I see you already took your reward."

"What?"

"This clip had $800 in it when I lost it."

They begin arguing, and eventually come before the rabbi.

Both state their case. The rich man concludes by saying, "Rabbi, I trust you believe me."

The rabbi says, "Of course," and the rich man, who's also a major donor to the synagogue, smiles.

The poor man is crushed.

Until the rabbi hands him the money.

"What are you doing?!" says the rich man.

The rabbi says, "You are, of course, an honest man, and you say the clip you lost had $800 in it. Therefore, I'm sure it did. But if the man who found this clip is a liar and a thief, he wouldn't have returned it. Therefore, this man did not remove $100 from it. And since this clip only contains $700, it must belong to somebody else. If that man steps forward, he'll get the money. Until then, it belongs to the man who found it."

"What about my money?" says the rich man.

"Well, we'll just have to wait until somebody finds a clip with $800 in it."

#112

COMPLAINING CONGREGANT

During his first service leading the community, the new rabbi sees an older congregant walk over to the synagogue president and demand rather loudly that the air conditioning be turned down because it's too cold.

The president nods kindly and takes care of it.

Just a few prayers later, the same congregant asks the president to turn the air conditioning up because it's too hot.

Not long after that, it's too cold again for the congregant. And then it's too hot.

On and on it goes, all morning long.

The president always nods kindly and takes care of it.

After services, the new rabbi says to the president, "I was very impressed with your patience in handling the individual who kept complaining about the air conditioner."

"No big deal. We don't have an air conditioner."

#113

3,000-YEAR-OLD MUMMY

A famous Israeli archaeologist was digging in the Negev when he discovers a mummy—a highly unusual occurrence.

He immediately calls the head of the Israel Museum in Jerusalem.

"I've just discovered a 3,000-year-old mummy who died of heart failure!"

"Bring him in. We'll have him examined."

A week later, the archaeologist is called in.

"You were right about the mummy's age *and* his cause of death! How on earth did you know?"

"My friend, I have thirty-five years' experience. And he was holding a parchment that said 10,000 shekels on Goliath."

#114

DEAR LORD, LEND ME STRENGTH!

"Dear Lord, so far today, I haven't gossiped, haven't lost my temper, haven't been greedy, grumpy, nasty, selfish, or over-indulgent.

"Thank you, Lord, for sending me the strength to do that.

"But in a few minutes, Lord, I'm going to need a lot more help, because I'm getting out of bed . . ."

#115

SHABBAT WITH THE MAYOR

To better understand his Jewish constituents, the mayor reaches out to a popular rabbi, and gets invited to spend Shabbat in his home.

The rabbi makes the kiddush blessing on Friday night over a full cup of wine.

After the fish, they make a l'chaim[23] with some fine scotch.

The main course comes with Israeli wine.

They recite the grace after the meal over another cup of wine.

The next day they make kiddush over wine at the synagogue.

After the service, they eat crackers with herring and make a few l'chaims with vodka.

They go home and the rabbi makes kiddush for his family over another cup of wine. They have a l'chaim with the fish, and another with the schnitzel. More wine follows with the grace after the meal.

And when Shabbat ends, they make the Havdalah blessing over another cup of wine.

_____

23 Toast to life!

The mayor turns to the rabbi.

"Thank you for sharing Shabbat with me! I had a wonderful time. I still don't get why you can't turn the lights on and off, but I do understand why you can't drive!"

#116

PRAYING FOR RAIN

Once in ancient Israel, it hadn't rained for months. Hunger was setting in, and the villagers were getting desperate.

The rabbi decreed that all the men would pray for rain on a nearby mountaintop.

They did, and . . . no rain.

They resolved to climb the mountain again the following day and bring their wives and children.

They all prayed together, and . . . no rain.

The following day they brought the old, the sick, and the babies.

Still no rain.

Next day, they brought along every chicken, goat, horse, and donkey in the village.

Still nothing.

The rabbi raised his eyes to the sky and said, "Why, G-d?! Why don't you heed our prayers?!"

A voice from Heaven answered, "BECAUSE YOU LACK FAITH!"

"How can you say that? We're all here praying our hearts out!"

"BUT DID ANY OF YOU BRING AN UMBRELLA?"

#117

THE DEBUTANTE BALL

It's 1958, and the captain of the US Navy base in Biloxi, Mississippi gets a call.

"Captain, my name is Amelia Ainsley. Of the Biloxi Ainsleys, as I'm sure you're aware?"

"I'm new to the area, ma'am."

"Well, Captain, when an Ainsley comes out at a debutante ball, it's quite the thing. And this is my daughter's year. I would like you to send over four young officers, handsome of course. Impeccably dressed, unmarried, and well-bred."

"I suppose we have some boys like that."

"They should expect an evening of polite conversation, proper dancing, and a bit of punch. No drunkenness. Oh, and Captain, I'm sure it goes without saying, no Jews. We surely don't appreciate Jews at an Ainsley affair."

"Copy that, ma'am. No Jews it is."

The night arrives, and Mrs. Ainsley opens the door of Ainsley Hall to find four handsome, impeccably dressed, African American naval officers on her porch.

"Uh . . . . uh . . . there must be some mistake!"

"No, ma'am, Captain Cohen doesn't make mistakes."

#118

A GOOD SERMON

The great George Burns said, "The secret to a good sermon is to have a good beginning and a good ending. And the two should be as close together as possible."

Amen, George!

#119

THE LEMON BET

Big John was the strongest man around. He was so sure of it, he had a standing bet.

He'd squeeze a whole lemon into a glass. Then he'd the hand the lemon to any challenger. If the man could squeeze out a single drop more, Big John would pay him 100 to 1.

Many people tried: weightlifters, rowers, wrestlers, boxers—but nobody could do it, and Big John made a tidy sum taking their bets.

One day, Sidney Wasserstein approached Big John in the pub, and laid a $100 bill on the bar.

Big John and his pals looked down at scrawny Sidney, all five feet two inches of him, and laughed.

"Happy to take your money, little fella."

A lemon was brought out, and Big John filled a whiskey glass with its juice.

Every patron in the pub chuckled as Big John handed the wrinkled peel to Sidney.

The smaller man wrapped his hands around it and squeezed.

Shock filled the room, as not one, but four drops fell into the glass!

Scowling, Big John pulled out his checkbook and asked, "What are you, a circus act or something?"

"Chairman of my synagogue's building fund."

#120

THE ROWING TEAM

Yeshiva University offers a new sport: rowing.

Unfortunately, the team loses one race after another. Though they train for hours every day, they always finish dead last.

Finally the team sends captain Tzvi Kepplestein to spy on Harvard, the perennial champions.

Tzvi drives up to Cambridge and rides his bicycle beside the Charles River. He watches the Harvard crew practice for a week, carefully taking notes.

Upon his return to Y.U., Tzvi gathers his teammates.

"I figured out their secret."

"Thank God! What is it? Tell us!"

"They have one guy yelling, and the other eight rowing!"

#121

FOUR NUNS

Four novice nuns are about to take their vows.

Dressed in white gowns, they enter the chapel for their symbolic marriage to Jesus.

Just as the ceremony is about to begin, four Hasidic Jews come in and sit in the front row.

The Mother Superior says, "I am so honored you want to share this experience with us. May I ask why you came?"

"We're from the groom's family."

#122

DRIVING THROUGH ISRAEL

A Texan driving through Israel begins to feel thirsty.

He sees a farmer picking oranges and pulls over.

"Can you give me a drink of water?"

The farmer obliges.

"Thank you so much! I needed that. So, how big is your spread?"

"Here in front, it's a good fifty meters, as you can see, and in the back we have close to a hundred meters of fine orange grove. And you?"

"Well, on my ranch, I can have breakfast, get in my car, drive all day, and I don't reach the end of my property until dinnertime."

"Yes, I know what you mean. I had a car like that too."

#123

AN EL AL HOLIDAY FLIGHT

As the late December flight lands at Ben Gurion airport, Captain Mizrahi makes an announcement.

"Welcome to Israel! Please remain seated with your seatbelt fastened until the aircraft comes to a complete stop. I repeat, do not stand up until the seat belt signs have been turned off.

"For those of you still in your seats, I wish you a very Merry Christmas!

"For those standing in the aisles, Happy Hanukkah!"

#124

THE PARKING SPOT

Meyer is late for an important meeting and can't find parking. Four times he circles the block to no avail.

"Please, God, please! Find me a parking spot and I'll give up gambling! And drinking! And lying! I'll go to synagogue on Shabbat! I'll even keep kosher!"

Immediately, a car pulls out in front of Meyer, and he zips into the open spot.

"Never mind, God! I found one!"

#125

TRY THE HAM

A rabbi and a priest meet at their town's Fourth of July picnic. Old friends, they begin their usual banter.

"This baked ham is so good. You really ought to try it. I know it's against your religion, but how could such a fine dish be forbidden! You don't know what you're missing. You simply haven't lived until you've tried Mrs. Smythe's baked ham. Tell me, Rabbi, when are you going to break down and have a bite?"

"At your wedding."

#126

SHABBOS WITH A NEW HUSBAND

A rabbi dies. After some time has passed, the congregation encourages his widow Sarah to marry again. The only candidate available is Shloimy the butcher. Sarah is reluctant because she's used to living with a scholar, but eventually she accepts, and they get married.

On their first Friday afternoon as husband and wife, Shloimy says, "My mother always said that before the start of Shabbat, it's a mitzvah to make love." So, they do.

After Shabbat dinner, Shloimy says, "My grandfather told me that one should always make love on Shabbos night." They do.

As soon as they awake in the morning, Shloimy tells Sarah, "My aunt says that a pious Jew always starts the Shabbos day by making love." And once again, they do.

On Sunday, Sarah goes out to the market. A friend rushes over and asks, "Nu, so how's the new husband?"

"An intellectual he's not, but he comes from a wonderful family!"

#127

LAST MEAL & TESTAMENT

Three prisoners of war—a Frenchman, an Italian, and a Jew—are condemned to execution.

"You may have one final meal before you die. Choose the menu."

The Frenchman says, "Fresh baked baguette, creamy camembert, juicy tomato, and cabernet sauvignon to wash it down."

He eats, and they execute him.

The Italian says. "Homemade penne rustica with marinara and a tart Chianti to wash it down."

He eats, and they execute him.

The Jew says, "I would like please a bowl of strawberries."

"Strawberries! They aren't in season!"

"Nu, so I'll wait."

#128

ARE YOU JEWISH?

A woman on the F train turns to the man next to her.

"Excuse me, but are you Jewish?"

"No."

A few minutes later she turns to him again.

"Are you sure you're not Jewish?"

"I'm sure."

A few more minutes go by.

"Are you absolutely sure you're not Jewish?"

"OK, fine. Yes, you're right. I'm Jewish."

"It's funny, because you don't look Jewish."

#129

DRIVING THE FAMILY CAR

The rabbi's son turns sixteen and asks to drive the family car.

"I'll make you a deal. If you get your grades up, set a regular schedule for Torah learning, and get a haircut, I'll let you use the car."

A month later, the boy goes to see his father.

"Dad, I got my grades up and I've been learning Torah regularly. Can I use the car?"

"What about the haircut?"

"I've been thinking about that. Samson in the Bible had long hair. Moses had long hair. Even Abraham had long hair."

"Yes, they did. And everywhere they went, they walked!"

#130

SHIMON'S NOT JEWISH

Shimon and Yankel are best friends and longtime learning partners.

One day, Shimon says, "I've got a confession to make: I'm not Jewish."

"What do you mean you're not Jewish? We've been learning Torah together for years!"

"I love the Torah and the commandments, and I love learning with you, but I'm not actually Jewish."

"You keep Shabbos! A non-Jew can't keep Shabbos."

"That's why I keep a key in my pocket every Shabbos."

"So what? We have an eiruv."

"I don't hold by the eiruv."[24]

---

24 If you didn't get this joke, don't feel bad. It's ridiculously Jewish, and Orthodox to boot. On Shabbos (Shabbat), Jews are not allowed to carry objects more than four cubits in the public domain. This prohibition can be circumvented if the community has an "eiruv," a symbolic boundary often made of fishing line strung along light poles and existing barriers like fences and walls, that serves to render a whole community like one piece of private property, thus allowing Jews to carry objects within it on Shabbos. Some Orthodox Jews are too strict to make use of this loophole, however, and they're the ones who say, "I don't hold by the eiruv."

#131

THE ATHEIST

A Jewish atheist and his family move to a new town where the best school is Catholic, so they send their son there.

Everything is fine until one day the boy comes home and tells his dad what he learned in school: all about the Father, the Son, and the Holy Spirit.

The atheist gets aggravated and says "Son, listen to me and listen good. There's only one God . . . and we don't believe in Him."

#132

FOUR BUBBIES

Four bubbies in Miami are having a nice afternoon playing cards. Eventually there's a lull in the conversation.

Finally, one of them sighs and says, "Oy."

The second one responds, "Oy vey."

The third exclaims, "Oy vey iz mir!"

And the fourth one says, "I thought we agreed not to talk about our children."

#133

THE LUMBERJACK

During the Great Depression a little Russian Jew applies for the only job available.

"Mr. Rabinowitz, you don't look like a lumberjack."

"Oh, I'm a very experienced lumberjack!"

"Yeah? Where did you work?"

"In the Sahara Forest!"

"You mean the Sahara Desert?"

"Sure, *now* it's a desert!"

#134

THE PRAYER

A newly minted rabbi from Cleveland takes over the pulpit of small synagogue in Chicago.

On his very first Shabbat, an argument breaks out among the congregants as to whether one should sit or stand during the Shema prayer.

On Sunday morning, the young rabbi visits Sol Glouberman in a nursing home.

"Mr. Glouberman, as the oldest member of the synagogue, please tell me, what is our custom during the Shema?"

"Why do you ask?"

"Because when we recited it yesterday, some people stood and some people sat. The ones who were standing yelled at the seated ones, telling them to stand up. And the ones who were sitting yelled back, telling the standing people to sit down."

"Ah, yes, *that* is our custom."

#135

THE BRISKET

A young mother is making brisket the day before Rosh Hashanah. Her little daughter watches with interest as she slices off the ends of the brisket before placing it in the roasting pan.

"Mommy, why do you cut off the ends?"

"You know, I'm not sure. This is the way Grandma always did it. Let's call her and ask."

"Hi, Sweetheart!"

"Hi, Mom. We were just wondering why you cut off the ends of the brisket before roasting?"

"Hmm. To be honest, I don't know. My mother always did it that way. Let's go visit her and ask."

"Oh, what a joy! My daughter, granddaughter, and great-granddaughter all on the same day!"

"Mama, we were just wondering why we cut the ends off the brisket before roasting?"

"Well, I don't know why you do it, but I never had a pan that was big enough."

#136

DRINKING IN THE MOUNTAINS

Four old friends go trekking in the Alps.

The Russian says, "I'm tired and thirsty. I must have vodka."

The German says, "I'm tired and thirsty. I must have beer."

The Frenchman says, "I'm tired and thirsty. I must have wine."

The Jew says, "I'm tired and I'm thirsty. I must have diabetes."

#137

THE FIRING SQUAD

Two Jews are standing in front of a firing squad.

The commandant says, "Any last requests?"

One of them says, "I would like please a blindfold."

The other one whispers, "Sam! Don't make trouble."[25]

---

25 I've had many jokes go viral on the @accidentaltalmudist page on
Instagram. This one was interesting because older Jews all get it, and
the younger ones often don't. As my father says, "The birth of modern Israel in 1948 changed our lives. Before that, we'd walk around
with our noses down, afraid to attract attention and the danger that
came with it. After 1948, we felt strong enough to walk around with
our heads up, proud and grateful to be Jewish."

#138

THE SEEING-EYE DOG

Sam and Charlie are walking their dogs past the synagogue one Saturday morning.

Sam says, "Let's go in. I hear they have great scotch in their kiddush club on Shabbos."

"They'll never let us in with the dogs."

"I got a plan. Follow my lead."

They enter and the gabbai[26] says, "No dogs allowed."

Sam says, "But it's my seeing-eye dog."

"Sorry, I didn't realize. OK, you can go in."

Charlie follows. Again the gabbai says, "Sorry, no dogs allowed."

"But it's my seeing-eye dog."

"A chihuahua is your seeing-eye dog?"

"Chihuahua?! Is that what they gave me?"

---

26 Akin to the rabbi's assistant.

#139

THE AIRPLANE PART

Boeing needs a new airplane part and receives three bids. A Polish company will deliver it for $3000, a British company for $6000, and an Israeli company will deliver it for $9000.

Given the wide discrepancy in bids, the man at Boeing in charge of the bidding decides to visit the factories.

In Poland, he meets the company CEO and asks, "How do you allocate your $3000 bid?"

"$1000 for materials, $1000 for labor, and $1000 for overhead, including a little profit for us."

In England, the man from Boeing asks the same question.

"$2000 materials, $2000 labor, and $2000 overhead, including some profit for us."

In Israel, the man from Boeing can't locate the factory. The address on the bid brings him to a residential building. An older Israeli answers the door.

The man from Boeing says, "Did you send us a bid for $9000?"

"Yes, I did."

"And how do you allocate that?"

"$3000 for me, $3000 for you, and $3000 for the schmuck in Poland."

#140

THE PRODIGAL SON RETURNS

Richard Goldstein grows up in New Haven, the son of prominent Yale professors. He becomes a rising scholar himself and is invited to give an important lecture before the entire Yale faculty—the final test before he's granted tenure alongside his parents.

On the biggest night of his life, he nervously places his notes on the podium . . . and they fall to the floor around him. As he bends down to pick them up, he passes gas explosively, and is mortified to hear the fart amplified by the PA system at wall-shaking level.

The audience gasps, and then suppresses its chuckles. Completely unnerved, Goldstein stammers through about half his speech before he gives up, runs off the stage, heads straight to his car, and roars off the Yale campus, never to return.

Many years later, his parents pass away, and he returns to tie up the estate. He's sitting at a sidewalk café reminiscing, when a young waiter brings his coffee.

"First time in New Haven?"

"Actually, I grew up here but I moved away."

"Do you visit often?"

"Not in years. Something happened, and I've been too embarrassed to return."

"Well, sir, I may not have your life experience, but one thing I have learned is that what seems embarrassing to me, most people don't even notice let alone remember. I bet that's true for your incident too."

"I suppose that's possible, but I doubt it."

"Was it a long time ago?"

"Oh, it's been decades."

"Before or after the Goldstein fart?"

#141

FEMME FATALE

Gary goes to the rabbi.

"Rabbi, my wife is trying to kill me."

"Gary, that's nonsense. You're married thirty-five years. A bunch of children, many more grandchildren. You're a model couple!"

"You don't know her like I do, Rabbi. I'm sure she's poisoning me. What do I do?"

"Gary, let me talk to her. I'll give her a call."

Next day, the rabbi calls Gary.

"OK, I called your wife and listened to her for three hours. My advice? Take the poison."

#142

DOUBLE POSITIVE

At the annual conference of the Comparative Language Society, a professor delivers the keynote address.

" . . . most of the world's languages employ a double negative to express a positive. For example, is this my favorite conference of the year? I'm not saying it isn't!"

Most of his fellow language mavens chuckle appreciatively.

"But we have found no language on earth that employs a double positive to express a negative."

From the back of the auditorium, Solly Horowitz can be heard scoffing, "Yeah, yeah."

#143

MEETING NEIL ARMSTRONG

A huge fan of the astronaut Neil Armstrong finally gets a chance to meet his idol at a book signing.

"Mr. Armstrong, I've always wanted to know, how did you come up with those epic words, 'One small step for man, one giant leap for mankind.' Did you plan it, or was it spontaneous?"

"To be honest, that's not what I said. The actual quote was, 'One small step for man, one giant leap for Manny Klein."

"Manny Klein? Who the heck is Manny Klein?"

"Years ago, when Mrs. Armstrong and I were starting out, we lived in an apartment building with very thin walls, and our neighbors were the Kleins. We heard everything that went on next door, including Manny's repeated request for a particular thing in the bedroom, to which Mrs. Klein would always respond, 'Manny, you'll get that when a man walks on the moon!'"

#144

THE NEW SUIT

Mendy goes to the tailor to try on his new custom suit. The first thing he notices is that the sleeves are too long.

The tailor says, "No problem, just bend your arms a bit at the elbow and hold them out in front of you. See, now the length is perfect."

"But the collar is too high."

"Nonsense, just hunch your back a little. A little more. That's it. Nice!"

"But I'm stepping on the pant cuffs."

"Oh, but you have to bend your knees a little. There. Now look in the mirror. The suit fits perfect! Like a custom suit should."

Knotted like a pretzel, Mendy shuffles out into the street.

Two ladies walking by take notice.

"Look at the poor man. I wonder if he was born that way?"

"Who knows? But thank God he found a suit that fits."[27]

---

27 This joke makes a good parable regarding the ways we slide into unhelpful and even self-destructive behaviors over time, and the great challenge of emerging from those patterns.

#145

LOST IN THE MALL

Max and Ruthie go to the biggest mall in America. After shopping all day, Ruthie realizes she's lost track of her husband.

Searching all over, she can't find him, so she calls frantically.

"Max, where are you? I've looked everywhere!"

"Ruthie, do you remember that jewelry store we visited years ago, and there was a pair of diamond earrings you fell in love with, and I said one day when I can afford it, I'll come back and get them for you?"

"Yes, Max, I remember. I remember!"

"OK, I'm in the sports bar right next to that store."

#146

A VISIT FROM THE KGB

In the darkest days of the Soviet Union, a KGB agent enters a ratty old building.

He walks up several flights of stairs and knocks on the door of a dingy apartment with a name plate that says DAVIDOVICH.

The KGB agent pounds on the door and finally an old man in a shabby coat opens it.

"Does Davidovich live here?"

"No."

"Who are you?"

"Davidovich."

"So why did you say Davidovich doesn't live here?"

"You call this living?"

#147

PASSOVER CLEANING

David Goldschlager goes to see his boss.

"We're doing some major house-cleaning tomorrow for Passover, and my wife needs me to help with the attic and the garage, moving, vacuuming, mopping, stacking and reorganizing. It's gonna take all day."

"Look, David, we're short-handed. I can't just give you the day off."

"Thanks, Boss. I knew I could count on you."

#148

WHAT'S IN A NAME?

Debbie Diamond takes her son to his first day of school.

"Bubbeleh, have a wonderful day at school! Oh, and bubbeleh, please be sure to eat all of the lunch I packed for you. I'll be waiting to pick you up as soon as school is over. I love you, bubbeleh!"

When school ends, Debbie is there.

"How was school, bubbeleh?"

"Good, Mommy."

"And what did you learn today?"

"I learned my name is Marvin."

#149

A DAY AT THE ZOO

A out-of-work actor named Ernie Schwartz reluctantly applies for a job as a gorilla impersonator. He's shocked to learn he'll be working at the Central Park Zoo, where budget cuts prevent the zoo from replacing the gorilla who recently died.

From nine to five, Ernie has to act like a gorilla while kids laugh and cheer. At first, he's humiliated, but after a while he begins to enjoy it. He's an entertainer after all, and the kids are entertained.

He starts swinging on the vines, eating bananas, and beating his chest with gusto, and before long he starts drawing big crowds.

One day, he loses his grip while swinging on a vine, and lands in the lion enclosure.

Staring into eyes of the king of beasts, a terrified Ernie manages to stammer out the Shema,[28] "*Hear, O Israel, the Lord our God, the Lord is One.*"

The lion growls back in Hebrew, "*Blessed be the name of His glorious kingdom forever.*"[29]

And from the next exhibit over, a grizzly bear hisses, "Will you two shut up? You're gonna get us all fired!"

---

28 When death seems certain, a Jew recites this prayer.
29 Second line of the Shema.

#150

THE SHIKSA

As Larry Green leaves for college, his father says goodbye.

"One last thing, son. Date only Jewish girls. If you date shiksas, you'll end up marrying one, and she'll only cause trouble."

Larry meets a beautiful blonde non-Jewish girl and falls in love. Eventually they decide to marry.

Larry tries to reassure his father that Katie is converting to Judaism, but it's no use. Even though the old man isn't religious, he furiously disapproves of his son marrying a gentile.

Larry and Katie marry anyway.

She takes her conversion seriously and becomes a pious Orthodox Jew. They have children.

Years later, Larry's father buys a boat and invites the whole family for a day of sailing.

Larry says, "Sorry, Dad, we can't come on Shabbos."

And his father answers, "Didn't I say the shiksa would cause trouble?"

#151

THE RACETRACK

A gust of wind blows a rabbi's hat off his head. A nice young man sprints after it and returns it to the rabbi.

"Thank you so much! I never would've caught it, and this hat belonged to my father. Young man, please accept this $20 as a token of my gratitude and may God shower you in blessings!"

"Wow, thank you so much, sir. But I can't take the $20."

"I insist."

They part company and the young man thinks to himself, "I've got $20, and a rabbi blessed me. This is my lucky day!"

He heads to racetrack and arrives just in time for the fifth race. A horse named Fedora is running.

"The rabbi's hat was a fedora! Must be a sign."

He bets the $20 at 20 to 1, and the horse wins. Now he's got $400. In the next race, there's a horse named Stetson.

"Another hat!"

He bets the $400 at 10 to 1 and wins. Now he's got $4000.

Later that night, he tells the story to his mom.

"In the next race, I bet it all on Panama at 15 to 1."

"Panama?"

"Like a Panama hat. And I won $60,000!"

"Oh my God, you have $60,000?"

"Actually, there was one more race, and there was an 8 to 1 horse in it named Chateau, so I put the $60K on him. But that nag came in dead last."

"Oh, son, chateau means castle! Chapeau is a hat! You had $60,000 and you threw it away!"

"Wouldn't have mattered anyway. The winning horse wasn't a hat. Just some Japanese horse named Yamaka."[30]

---

30 Yarmulke, often pronounced yamaka, is Yiddish for the skullcap worn by Jewish men.

#152

THE HOTLINE

The President visits the Pope.

After the photos, they have coffee in the Pope's office and the President notices a bright red phone.

"What's that for?"

"Hot line to God."

"Really? How much does a call cost?"

"Million dollars a minute, and worth every penny."

The President continues his trip and meets with the Prime Minister of Israel. When he arrives, the P.M. is speaking on a red phone like the Pope's.

He whispers, "I'll be off as soon as I can. Talking with God."

Ten minutes later, the Prime Minister hangs up.

"Sorry about that. We have a lot going on here, and I needed to check in with the Boss. He sends His regards."

"Wow. Must be nice. But that call must've cost ten million dollars."

"No, about seventy-five cents."

"But in the Vatican, the Pope . . ."

"From here it's a local call."

#153

THE NEW RESTAURANT

In a Florida retirement community, Jake and Ed chat by the barbecue while their wives mix drinks inside.

"Last night we discovered a spectacular new restaurant. Food to die for. Portions so big, the doggie bag's a whole other dinner. And didn't cost much at all. Best deal in Miami."

"Wow, what's it called?"

"It's called . . . uh . . . you know, what's the name of the flower with red petals and thorns?"

"Rose?"

"Right, Rose."

He turns toward the house.

"Rose! What's the name of that restaurant we ate at last night?"

#154

HEAVENLY LINKS

Moses, Jesus, and God are playing golf. On the first tee Moses slices his drive into the lake.

He walks over, raises his arm, and the waters part. He steps into the lakebed, hits a beautiful approach shot onto the green and makes the putt for birdie.

On the next hole, Jesus hooks his drive into the lake. He walks on the water and lifts his hand. The ball floats to the surface. He hits a beauty onto the green and makes the putt for birdie.

On the third hole, God slices his drive into the lake. As the ball sinks in the water, a fish darts over and swallows it. Then an eagle swoops into the lake and grabs the fish in its talons. As the eagle bends to eat the fish, it disgorges the golf ball, which drops into a tree, bounces from branch to branch and finally falls on the green, where it rolls into the cup for a hole-in-one.

Moses turns to God and says, "Are You gonna keep screwing around or are we gonna play golf?"

#155

DOG GONE

Lily, a sweet old lady, boards an El Al flight to Israel with her backpack and a little dog carrier that she places on the adjoining seat.

The flight attendant says, "I'm sorry, but your dog can't ride here. I'll have to put it in the pets compartment."

Lily reluctantly agrees.

During the flight, the attendant looks in on the little dog and is horrified to discover the animal died. In a panic she tells the captain who notifies El Al in Tel Aviv. Fearing a PR disaster, they get an exact description of the dead dog and buy a replacement.

When the plane lands, Lily goes to the baggage desk for her carrier and sees the exact replica of her dog inside.

"That's not my dog."

"Of course it is. Same color, same collar."

"That is not my dog."

"How can you say this isn't your dog?"

"Because my dog is dead."

#156

STRANDED

Gil and Hedy are flying to Fiji for their fiftieth wedding anniversary. A sudden storm knocks out the plane's engines and they're forced to make an emergency water landing.

They wash up on the beach of a desert island. No sign of human habitation anywhere.

Hedy panics.

"No one will ever find us here! Gil, we're going to die on this island!"

"Hedy, did you send the check for our pledge to the United Jewish Appeal?"

"No, I forgot. I'm sorry."

Gil's face lights up.

"Don't worry, Hedy. They'll find us!"

#157

NOW HEAR THIS

Ned and Larry sit by the pool in Boca Raton.

"I just got a new hearing aid. Cost a fortune, and worth every penny. I can hear everything. Those people talking by the deep end. Waiter tapping his pencil. That seagull breathing. Everything."

"Wow. What kind is it?"

"A quarter to three."

#158

DUE IN THE MORNING

Nina wakes up in the middle of the night to find her husband pacing the floor.

"What's the matter, Joel?"

"I borrowed $1000 from your cousin Sam. It's due in the morning and I don't have the money. I don't know what I'm going to do."

Nina picks up the phone and dials.

"Hi Sam, it's Nina . . . Yes, I realize it's three o'clock in the morning, but you know that $1000 Joel owes you? He doesn't have it. Bye!"

She hangs up.

"Now you get some sleep and let him worry."

#159

THE BIG GAME

Yankel calls his rabbi.

"I know tonight is Yom Kippur, and Kol Nidre's the most important service of the year. But it's also Game 7 of the World Series. Rabbi, the Dodgers are in it! I gotta watch the game on TV."

"Yankel, that's what your DVR is for."

"Really? I can tape Kol Nidre?"

#160

THE BALL GAME

Morrie and Irv are lifelong Yankees fans who've been attending games together for decades. One frequent topic of conversation is whether there's baseball in heaven. The friends agree that whoever dies first will find a way to send a message from the next world and answer this question.

One day in the middle of baseball season, Irv has a massive heart attack and dies. The night after his funeral, he appears to Morrie in a dream.

"Irv is that really you??"

"Yes, Morrie, it's me."

"Wow, I can't believe this is happening! OK, Irv, do they have baseball in heaven?"

"Morrie, I have good news and bad news. Which do you want first?"

"Tell me the good news."

"OK, the answer is yes. There's baseball in heaven!"

"That's fantastic! So what could be the bad news?"

"You're pitching tomorrow."

#161

WE NEED YOU NOW, STANLEY!

Stanley is having coffee in his mansion when there's a knock at the door. It's the rabbi.

"Stanley, we have a very important initiative at the synagogue. It's a preschool, and it will ensure our future. We need your help, Stanley, and in a *significant* way."

"Rabbi, I have a kid in college; he wants to go to law school. I have another kid in college; she wants to go to medical school. I've got a cousin on the verge of bankruptcy; he needs a bridge loan or his whole life is gonna fall apart, and I have an aunt who needs a lifesaving operation. So, Rabbi, if I could say no to them, I can say no to you."

#162

SILENT DEBATE

In a medieval city, the bishop decides all Jews have to leave. They cry out in protest and get support from a few nobles, so the bishop proposes a religious debate with a Jew. If the Jew wins, they can all stay. If he loses, off with his head and the rest leave.

That night, the Jews are in tears. No one wants to debate the bishop, who's also a famous theologian. Finally, Yitzy the Stutterer volunteers. The rest of the Jews start packing.

On the big day, Yitzy says to the bishop, "E-e-e-veryone knows how b-b-b-brilliant you are, Your Eminence, and I'm j-j-j-just a simple Jew with s-s-s-stutter. So, let us d-d-d-debate in s-s-s-silence."

"Very well."

The bishop and Yitzy sit in two chairs facing one another, with hundreds of people watching. For a full minute they sit in silence, tension gripping the arena.

Then, the bishop raises his hand and shows three fingers.

Yitzy stares back and slowly raises one finger.

The bishop waives his hand in a circle around his head.

Yitzy points his finger at the ground.

The bishop beckons to an assistant, who brings him a wafer and a glass of wine. He shows these to Yitzy.

Yitzy pulls out an apple.

The bishop says, "He wins. The Jews can stay."

That night in the cathedral, the bishop's students ask him what happened.

"I had to concede, the man was too good. First, I held up three fingers to declare the Trinity. He responded with one finger for the one God common to all of us. I waved my hand around my head to show him that God is everywhere. He pointed to the ground to say God is not in some ambiguous 'everywhere.' God is here, now, watching our debate. So, I asked for the wine and wafer to show that God absolves me from sin. And that seemingly simple man pulled out an apple to remind me of Original Sin. He had an answer for everything. What could I do?"

Meanwhile, the Jews crowd around Yitzy the Stutterer at the victory party, begging to know it all meant.

"Well, f-f-first he said the J-J-Jews have three days to g-g-get out. I told him not a s-s-s-single one of us is leaving. He t-t-told me that this whole city would be c-c-c-cleared of J-J-J-Jews. I s-s-s-said I'm staying r-r-r-right here!"

"And then . . . ?"

"N-n-n-no idea. He took out his lunch, so I took out mine."

ACKNOWLEDGMENTS

I wrote one of the jokes in this book—the other 161 I adapted from the priceless treasure I inherited: our Jewish humor tradition, and I thank my ancestors for that.

Here's one more, and it's the oldest recorded joke on Earth:

Because there are no graves in Egypt you brought us out here to die in the desert?[31]

It's not hilarious, but its tone is spot on, and a modern Jew might say these very words if thrust into the desert without food, water, or air conditioning among a vast crowd of compatriots. Special thanks to Moses for jotting it down during a free moment between complaints.

A thousand years later, the Talmud recorded that before teaching Torah, the great sage Rabbah would open with a joke, and his students would laugh.[32] So I'm just another link in the chain. I share Torah with a large online audience every day at *Accidental Talmudist*, and I learned early on that a little humor would help the Torah travel much further.

That is to say, *we* learned.

The Torah I share, the movies I direct, and the book in your hands are all shaped by the creativity, wisdom, wit,

---

31 Exodus 14:11.
32 Shabbos 30b, B. Talmud.

and counsel of my wife and writing partner, Nina. She's a genuine woman of valor,[33] and nothing I accomplish would be possible without her.

Our first viral post at facebook.com/accidentaltalmudist was joke #111. Now we have over a million followers.

We've collected Jewish jokes at accidentaltalmudist.org/humor for years and eventually I started telling them in videos on Instagram and TikTok. Hundreds of thousands of new followers joined us, and I thank every one of them, especially those who commented on the jokes, whether positively or negatively, for helping me to craft the best version of every joke.

The viral jokes brought us to the attention of Charlie Lyons. He saw the potential for a book and brought the idea to Tony Lyons, head of Skyhorse Publishing. Huge thanks to them for believing in this project. And big thanks to my editor Isaac Morris—he's sharp, creative, and a delight to work with.

Infinite thanks to Horatio Kemeny for inspiring me to aim higher and execute better for decades. You're the best!

And finally, I thank my boys in the Friday golf group, Josh Moorvitch, Eli Scharf, and Richie Gano, as well as our bartender Sarah Ferreira, for shushing the onlookers, turning off the music, holding the camera, and laughing heartily at the weekly joke . . . even if I have tell it three times to get it right!

---

33 Proverbs 31:1.

ABOUT THE AUTHOR

Salvador Litvak was born in Chile and grew up in New York. As a gangly Jewtino redhead, he always identified with outsiders and iconoclasts.

Sal directs movies. His latest is *Guns & Moses*, the story of a beloved small-town rabbi who becomes an unlikely gunslinger after his community is violently attacked, starring Mark Feuerstein, Neal McDonough, Alona Tal, Christopher Lloyd, and Dermot Mulroney.

Sal also directed the Passover comedy and cult classic, *When Do We Eat?*, the uplifting tale of a seder gone horribly awry, starring Max Greenfield, Ben Feldman, Shiri Appleby, Michael Lerner, Lesley Ann Warren, and Jack Klugman in his final role.

Sal writes with his wife and creative partner, Nina Litvak. Together they run *Accidental Talmudist*, a Jewish wisdom, humor, and history platform that reaches millions.

Sal graduated from Harvard, NYU Law, and UCLA Film.

His golf game needs work, but he's coached multiple gold medal teams at the Maccabiah Games in Israel, proving the old adage about those that can't do . . .

For public appearances, or to suggest a great Jewish joke for the next edition, reach out via salvadorlitvak.com.